A DICTIONARY OF SELECTED NOUNS FOR ALL AGES

ASHWANNIE HARRIPERSAUD

ASHMINI PRASAD CLINTON WARDE ANDREA RAMNAUTH

BLUEROSE PUBLISHERS
India | U.K.

Copyright © Ashwannie Harripersaud, Ashmini Prasad,
Clinton Warde, Andrea Ramnauth 2023

All rights reserved by the author. No part of this publication may be reproduced, stored in a retrieval system or transmitted in any form or by any means, electronic, mechanical, photocopying, recording or otherwise, without the prior permission of the author. Although every precaution has been taken to verify the accuracy of the information contained herein, the publisher assumes no responsibility for any errors or omissions. No liability is assumed for damages that may result from the use of information contained within.

BlueRose Publishers takes no responsibility for any damages, losses, or liabilities that may arise from the use or misuse of the information, products, or services provided in this publication.

For permissions requests or inquiries regarding this publication,
please contact:

BLUEROSE PUBLISHERS
www.BlueRoseONE.com
info@bluerosepublishers.com
+91 8882 898 898
+4407342408967

ISBN: 978-93-6261-409-4

Cover design: Tahira
Typesetting: Tanya Raj Upadhyay

First Edition: March 2024

BACKGROUND

A Dictionary of Selected Nouns for All Ages is a comprehensive reference tool that focuses solely on nouns. It is designed to provide users with a wealth of information on nouns and their various forms, meanings, and usage in the English language.

A Dictionary of Selected Nouns for All Ages features an extensive collection of over 2000 nouns, each of which is meticulously researched and defined. Entries include not only the noun's definition but also its various forms, pronunciation, and examples of usage in context.

This dictionary is organised alphabetically, making it easy to find specific nouns and their meanings. In addition to its thorough noun coverage, this dictionary also includes supplementary material to help users enhance their understanding of nouns and their usage. This includes a guide to noun types as well as guidance on how to use nouns correctly in sentences.

This dictionary was created by a team of four teachers of English who recognized the need for a specialized resource that specifically caters to nouns. Whether you are a student, writer, translator, or language enthusiast, this dictionary will provide you with the information you need to communicate effectively and express yourself with precision and clarity.

AIM

The aim of this dictionary is to provide an extensive and reliable resource for nouns in the English language. It seeks to cover a complete family of nouns, including common nouns, proper nouns, countable nouns, uncountable nouns, abstract nouns, and concrete nouns. This dictionary provides clear definitions, accurate spellings, and detailed examples of the usage and context of each noun. By focusing solely on nouns, this dictionary aims to offer a specialised and in-depth resource for anyone looking to expand their vocabulary and deepen their understanding of the English language.

SCOPE

A Dictionary of Selected Nouns for All Ages intends to cover as many nouns as possible from different fields, including but not limited to science, technology, art, history, culture, and everyday life.

This dictionary is intended to be user-friendly and accessible, providing clear and concise definitions and examples and using simple language wherever possible. It includes clear and consistent formatting, including pronunciation guides.

The goal of this dictionary is to provide a reliable and thorough resource for anyone looking to better understand and use nouns in their writing and communication.

RATIONALE

A dictionary that focuses specifically on nouns can be a valuable resource for anyone seeking to expand their vocabulary and understanding of language. Nouns are an essential part of any language, as they are the words used to identify and describe people, places, things, and ideas.

By creating a dictionary that focuses exclusively on nouns, readers can quickly and easily look up words that they may encounter in their reading or writing. This can be particularly helpful for students learning English as a second language, as they can focus on building their vocabulary of essential nouns before moving on to more complex grammar and syntax.

Furthermore, a noun-focused dictionary can provide more detailed and comprehensive definitions of nouns than a general-purpose dictionary. This can be especially helpful for technical or specialised fields where precise and accurate language is essential.

A dictionary that focuses on nouns can also help promote a deeper understanding and appreciation of language itself. By exploring the many nuances and meanings of nouns, readers can develop a greater understanding of the power and beauty of words and the vital role they play in communication and expression.

DEFINITION OF A NOUN

A noun is a term that refers to people, places, things, or ideas. They are a fundamental part of language and serve as the building blocks for communication. Nouns can be concrete, such as a dog or a car, or abstract, such as love or freedom.

Types of Nouns

1. *Common Nouns*

Common nouns are general names given to people, places, things, or ideas that belong to a group or class. They are not capitalised unless they appear at the beginning of a sentence. Examples of common nouns include "bag", "pencil", "book", "city", and "person". They are used to refer to everyday objects and concepts that are not specific or unique. They are often used in sentences as the subject, object, or complement.

2. *Proper Nouns*

Proper nouns are specific names given to particular people, places, or things and are always capitalized. Proper nouns refer to unique individuals, specific locations, or unique entities. Examples of proper nouns include names of people such as "John", "Mary", and "Michael", names of places such as "Berbice", "Georgetown", and "Guyana", and names of unique things such as "Coco-Cola", "Nike", and "Samsung". Proper nouns are used to distinguish one particular entity from others and to give them a unique identity. They are often used in sentences as the subject, object, or complement.

3. *Singular Nouns*

Singular nouns are words that refer to one person, place, thing, or idea. They are used to denote a single entity and are often modified by singular determiners such as "**a**", "**an**", or "**the**". Examples of singular nouns include "book", "table", "idea", and "city". Singular nouns can also be modified by adjectives or other words to provide more information or context. When using singular nouns in sentences, it is important to use singular verb forms, such as "**is**" or "**has**", to agree with the singular subject.

4. ***Plural Nouns***

Plural nouns are words that refer to two or more people, places, things, or ideas. They are used to denote more than one entity and are often modified by plural determiners such as "**many**", or "**several**", or by specific numerical quantifiers such as "**two**", "**three**", or "**ten**". Examples of plural nouns include "books", "tables", "ideas", and "cities". Plural nouns can also be modified by adjectives or other words to provide more information or context. In sentences, it is important to use plural verb forms, such as "**are**" or "**have**", to agree with the plural subject.

5. ***Concrete Nouns***

Concrete nouns are words that refer to physical objects or things that can be perceived by the senses. They are tangible and can be seen, touched, heard, tasted, or smelled. Examples of concrete nouns include "chair", "table", "dogs", "tree", and "apples". Concrete nouns can be both singular and plural.

6. ***Abstract Nouns***

Abstract nouns are words that refer to concepts, ideas, or emotions that cannot be perceived by the senses and are intangible. They represent qualities or characteristics that are not physical or concrete, such as "love", "happiness", "courage", "justice", or "freedom". Abstract nouns are often formed from adjectives, verbs, or other nouns by adding suffixes such as "**-ness**", "**-ment**", "**-ion**", "**-ity**", or "**-hood**". In sentences, abstract nouns can be used as the subject, object, or complement.

7. ***Collective Nouns***

Collective nouns are words that refer to a group of people, animals, or things. They are singular in form but refer to multiple entities. Collective nouns can be used for different groups, such as "a herd of cows", "a pack of wolves", "a swarm of bees", or "a team of players". In sentences, collective nouns can be used as the subject, object, or complement. It is important to use appropriate verbs and pronouns that agree with the singular form of the collective noun when using it as a subject. For example, "The **team is** playing well" instead of "The team is [are] playing well".

8. *Compound Nouns*

Compound nouns are words that are made up of two or more words that are combined to create a new word with a new meaning. Compound nouns can be formed by joining two nouns: a noun and an adjective, a noun and a verb, or a noun and a preposition, among other combinations. Examples of compound nouns include "sunflowers", "toothbrush", "firefighters", "basketball", "headteacher,", "post office", and "blackboard". Compound nouns can be written as one word, hyphenated, or as separate words. Compound nouns can be both singular and plural.

9. *Countable Nouns*

Countable nouns are nouns that can be counted as individual units or discrete items. They refer to things that can be quantified as one, two, three, and so on. Examples of countable nouns include "book", "dog", "apple", and "chair". Countable nouns can be both singular and plural, and they are often modified by numerals, such as "one book", or "two chairs", or by plural determiners, such as "**many**" or "**several**". In sentences, countable nouns can be used as the subject, object, or complement.

10. *Uncountable Nouns*

Uncountable nouns are nouns that cannot be counted as individual units or discrete items. They refer to things that are considered as a whole or in a mass. Examples of uncountable nouns include "water", "music", and "sand." Uncountable nouns are usually singular in form, and they do not have a plural form. Instead, they are modified by words like "**some**", "**a lot of**", or "**a little bit of**". In sentences, uncountable nouns can be used as the subject, object, or complement.

Gender of Nouns

1. *Masculine*

This gender is used for male beings, animals, and things that are considered masculine or have masculine traits. For example, "boy", "man", "bull", "king", and "father" are usually classified as masculine nouns.

2. *Feminine*

This gender is used for female beings, animals, and things that are considered feminine or have feminine traits. For example, "girl", "woman", "cow", "queen", and "mother" are usually classified as feminine nouns.

3. *Common*

This gender is used for nouns that do not have a specific gender and can refer to both male and female beings and things. For example, "teacher", "doctor", "friend", and "person" are usually classified as common gender nouns.

4. *Neuter*

This gender is used for things that are considered neither masculine nor feminine, such as objects, concepts, and abstract ideas. For example, "book", "tree", "love", and "freedom" are usually classified as neuter gender nouns.

डॉ. के. जे. श्रीनिवास
Dr. K.J. Srinivasa

भारतीय उच्चायुक्त
जॉर्जटाउन, गयाना
High Commissioner of India
Georgetown, Guyana

FOREWORD

Dear Reader,

Greetings form the High Commission of India in Guyana. I welcome you to this "Dictionary of Selected Nouns for all Ages".

Nouns are a diverse group of words, that are very common in English and help in defining people, items, space and places. With the wide varieties of nouns in English language, it becomes imperative to understand the usage, meanings, as well as their specificity which contributes in turn to a holistic understanding of the language.

This Dictionary featuring an extensive 2000 nouns, has been meticulously researched by the four authors, includes not only the definitions, but also the various forms, pronunciations and examples of usage in context for each noun. The guide to noun types will act as a suitable pilot for users on how to use the nouns correctly in sentences. This book is also intended to be used as a supplementary material, which, despite the abundance of dictionaries available, will concentrate on the single part of speech NOUNS.

Precision and clarity of this Dictionary will serve as an essential resource for English language learners to help in improving their writing skills, language fluency, as well as their vocabulary, implying an effective communication and expression by the user which oozes clarity and precision.

As a student, as a teacher, or as a writer, this Dictionary would provide a valuable, specialized and in-depth resource. The good deal of research by the team of 4 authors who are themselves teachers of English, would provide a user-friendly accessible source of language usage and help in clear communication – both verbal and in writing.

We hope that this Dictionary becomes a truly dependable and necessary tool for your progress and journey with the English language. I hope your foundation of English improves with this book and you can expand your horizons, unleashing the power of words.

Best Wishes to all the users of this book.

(Dr. K. J. Srinivasa)
21 May 2023

307 Church & Peter Rose Streets, Queenstown, Georgetown,
Guyana, Tel: 592-2263996/8965/3240   Fax: 592-2257012
Email: hc.georgetown@mea.gov.in
Website: www.hcigeorgetown.gov.in

Aa

aardvark /ˈɑrdˌvɑrk/
South African anteater with long ears and snout.
Example: The aardvark in the zoo is playful.

abacus /ˈæbəkəs/
a counting device consisting of a frame holding beads on metal rods.
Example: An abacus is a useful tool in learning arithmetic operations.

abalone /ˌæbəˈloni/
an edible sea creature with a shell lined with mother-of-pearl.
Example: This gigantic abalone was found on the beach.

abbacy /ˈæbəsi/
the office of an abbot or abbess.
Example: After years of dedicated service, the abbot was appointed to the abbacy.

abbess /ˈɑbɛs/
the nun in charge of a convent.
Example: During times of crisis, the abbess played a vital role in protecting the abbey.

abbey /ˈɑbi/
a church associated with a community of monks or nuns.
Example: This abbey is preserved as a fascinating historical site.

abbot /ˈɑbʌt/
the head of an abbey of monks.
Example: The abbot was well-respected within the community.

abdomen /ˈɑbdʌmən/
the part of the body that contains the stomach and intestines.

Example: Ulcers usually affect the abdomen.

aberration /ˌabəˈreɪʃən/

a sudden change from what is normal or accurate.

Example: The typos found in the BACKSPACE dictionary were an aberration from their consistent high standard of editing and proofreading.

a brief lapse in control of one's thoughts or feelings.

Example: The teacher's inappropriate comment was an aberration of judgment.

abeyance /əbeɤəns/

put aside temporarily.

Example: Investments are usually placed in abeyance when market conditions are unfavourable.

ability /ɑbˈɪlɪi/

possession of the necessary skill to do something.

Example: Your ability to solve complex mathematical problems is remarkable.

ablation /ˌɑbleɪʃən/

the surgical removal of an organ or body part.

Example: Ablation of hair follicles is a cosmetic treatment for hair removal.

the wearing away of a rock or glacier.

Example: The ablation of limestone cliffs destroys natural habitats.

ablution /ɑbluʃən/

the act of washing.

Example: I always take a quick ablution after returning from the gym.

abnormality /ˌæbnɔːˈmælətɪ/

an abnormal feature, characteristic, or occurrence.

Example: The auditors discovered an abnormality in the company's accounting policies.

abode /əˈboʊd/
one's home.
Example: My abode is small and cosy.

abolition /ˌæbəlɪʃən/
the act of doing away with something.
Example: The abolition of the death penalty has remained a controversial topic.

aborigine /ˌæbərɪdʒəni/
an original inhabitant of a country or region.
Example: As an Australia's aborigine, she has all rights as everyone else does.

abortion /æbɔrʃən/
an operation to end a pregnancy.
Example: The young woman decided to have an abortion as she was not financially stable to raise a child alone.

the failure of a mission or project.
Example: The abortion of the original proposal was inevitable because of group members' dependency.

abracadabra /ˌæbrækəˈdæbrə/
a word used in magic spells, which is supposed to possess magic powers.
Example: Medieval physicians' abracadabra were used to treat illnesses.

abrasion /æbreɪʃən/
a scraped area on the skin.
Example: The hiker had a long abrasion on her leg.
the erosion of rock-by-rock fragments.

Example: The Grand Canyon was formed due to the gradual abrasion of rocks by the Colorado River.

abscess /ɑbsɛs/
a swelling containing pus because of inflammation.
Example: The abscess on my leg is painful.

absence /ɑbsɛns/
the state of being away
Example: Your absence does not affect me any longer.
the fact of being without something.
Example: The absence of food in war-torn countries is a primary cause of severe humanitarian crises.

absentee /ˌɑbsɛnti/
a person who should be present but is not.
Example: John was labelled as an absentee during the team meeting.

absenteeism /ˌɑbsɛnˈtiːzəm/
persistent absence from work or school
Example: Many schools are implementing policies to discourage absenteeism.

absolution /ˌɑbsəˈłuʃən/
formal forgiveness of a sin pronounced by a priest
Example: The priest gave absolution to the sincere penitent after hearing his confession.

absolutism /ɑbsəlutɪzəm/
a political system in which a monarch, or dictator has unrestricted power
Example: Those who supported the throne of absolutism are highly favoured.

absorption /ɑbsɔrbʃən/
the process of absorbing something

Example: The absorption of water by the roots is essential for the plant's growth.

abstention /ɑbstɛntʃən/

the formal act of not voting

Example: The oppositions' abstention from the vote distant them from a controversial bill.

the act of abstaining from something

Example: My doctor recommended abstention from cigarettes to improve my health.

abstinence /ɑbstənɛns/

the practice of choosing not to do something one would like

Example: Abstinence is the most effective method of birth control.

abstraction / ɑbstrækʃən/

a general idea instead of a specific example.

Example: They do not engage in abstraction or analysis.

abundance /ɑbʌndəns/

a great amount

Example: The abundance of rainfall has led to severe flooding in many regions.

abuse /əbjus/

prolonged ill-treatment of or violence toward someone

Example: Shelters should be provided for all victims of abuse.

abyss /ɑbɪs/

a very deep hole in the ground

Example: The Grand Canyon is a massive abyss.

a frightening or threatening situation

Example: After her relationship fell apart, she felt like she was falling into an abyss of hopelessness.

acacia /ɑkeɪʃə/

a shrub or tree with small yellow or white flowers

Example:　　Many pollinators are drawn to the sweet nectar of the acacia.

academy /ɑkɑdəmi/

a society for the advancement of literature, art, or science

Example:　　She gave an address to the Royal academy.

a school for training in a particular skill

Example:　　This academy of music will hone your musical abilities.

acceleration /ɑksɛlɛrɛʃən/

the act of increasing speed or the rate of change of velocity

Example:　　Everything falls because of the acceleration due to gravity.

accelerator /ɑksɛlɚ-retɚ/

a pedal in a motor vehicle that is pressed to increase speed

Example:　　She slammed on the accelerator to beat the red light.

accent /ˈɑksɛnt/

the distinctive style of pronunciation of a person or group from a particular area

Example:　　Her French accent attracts everyone's attention.

a mark used in writing to indicate the prominence of a syllable or the way a vowel is pronounced

Example:　　In Spanish, the accent marks indicate the stress and tone of certain words.

acceptance /ɑksɛptəns/

the act of accepting something

Example:　　She was elated by the news of her acceptance at her dream university.

access /ˈɑksɛs/

a means of entering a place

Example: It is difficult to gain access into the mansion.

accession /əksɛʃən/

the act of taking up an office or position

Example: After the CEO's sudden death, the company had to expedite the accession of a CEO.

accessory /akˈsɛsɛri/

a supplementary part

Example: A phone case is an important accessory to protect your phone from damage.

a small item worn or carried by someone to complete his or her outfit

Example: Sunglasses can be a stylish accessory that protects your eyes.

a person who is involved in a crime but who was not present when it took place

Example: The driver was charged as an accessory to the robbery.

accident /ˈaksɪdɛnt/

an unpleasant event that causes damage, injury, and or death

Example: Five students were injured in the accident.

acclamation /ˌaklə'meɪʃən/

an enthusiastic reception or display of approval

Example: The champion athlete received acclamation from the crowd.

an instance of being elected without opposition

Example: The politician won the election by acclamation.

accolade /akəled/

an award or prize

Example: I received an accolade for my contribution to the field of science.

accommodation /akʌmədeʃən/

a place in which to sleep, live, or work

Example: The tour guides emphasised that tourists need to pay separately for their accommodation.

accompaniment /əkəmpnimɛnt/

something that accompanies something else

Example: The recipe serves as an excellent accompaniment to ice-cream.

a supporting part for an instrument, a band, or an orchestra

Example: The guitar provided a beautiful accompaniment to the singer's voice.

accompanist /əkəmpənəst/

a person who plays a musical accompaniment

Example: The guitarist is a talented accompanist who plays for many renowned singers.

accomplice /akɔmplɪs/

a person who helps someone else commit a crime

Example: Simon was sentenced to prison for robbery, and his accomplice was also arrested and charged with the same crime.

accomplishment /əkʌmplɪʃmɛnt/

the successful completion of something

Example: Messi's greatest accomplishment is winning the World Cup.

accord /akɔrd/

a formal agreement between groups or nations

Example: The two war-torn nations signed an accord to cease the bombing and begin peace talks.

accordance /akɔrdəns/

conforming to or according to

Example: The teacher graded the essays in accordance with the rubric.

accordion /ɑkɔrdiən/

a box-shaped musical instrument played by moving the two sides apart and together, and pressing a keyboard to produce the notes

Example: My sister plays her accordion for us on family gatherings.

account /ɐkaʊnt/

report or discussion

Example: This is an interesting account of the current wars around the world.

a person's money kept in a bank

Example: My pay cheques are deposited in my savings account.

accountant /əkaʊntənt/

a person who maintains and audits business accounts

Example: I am an aspiring accountant.

accoutrements /ɑkutrəmənts/

clothing and equipment for a particular activity

Example: The hiker acquired all the necessary accoutrements for her trip.

accretion /əkriʃən/

a gradual increase in size, through growth or addition

Example: Scientists believe that the accretion of dust and gas forms new stars and planets.

accumulation /ɑkjumjuleʃən/

something that has been collected

Example: The accumulation of pollutants in the water areas is becoming a major problem.

accumulator /əkjumjəuletə/

a rechargeable device for storing electrical energy

Example: Some heavy machineries use a hydraulic accumulator.

a collective bet on successive races, with both stake and winnings being carried forward to accumulate progressively

Example: He is an avid accumulator of financial data.

accuracy /ˈakjurɛsi/

faithful representation of the truth

Example: The accuracy of the financial statements was impressive.

accusation /ˌakjəˈzeʃən/

an allegation that a person is guilty of some wrongdoing

Example: The treasurer resigned after the allegation of embezzlement.

acetate /ˈasəˌtet/

any salt or ester of acetic acid

Example: The production of paint requires vinyl acetate.

acetone /ˈasəˌtoʊn/

a strong-smelling colourless liquid used as a solvent for paints and lacquers

Example: I must purchase a bottle of acetone.

acetylene /əˈsɛtəlin/

a colourless soluble flammable gas used in welding metals

Example: The welder uses acetylene to cut the thick metals.

achievement /əˈtʃivmɛnt/

something that has been accomplished by hard work, ability, or heroism

Example: The invention of the lightbulb was a great achievement.

the successful completion of something

Example: Marisa felt a sense of achievement after completing her assignments.

acid /ˈasɪd/

one of a class of compounds, corrosive and sour when dissolved in water, that combine with a base to form a salt

Example: The lab assistant instructed us to not touch the acid.

acidity /ɑsɪdəti/

the quality of being acid

Example: The lemon juice's acidity made the dish taste sour.

acid rain /ˈɑsɪd, ˈreɪn/

containing pollutants released into the atmosphere by the burning of coal or oil

Example: Acid rain damages stony and metallic buildings.

acid rock /ɑsɪd, ˈrɔk/

igneous rock with a silica content of more than two thirds and containing not less than ten per cent quartz

Example: The geography teacher gave each group an acid rock.

acid test /ɑsɪd, ˈtɛst/

a rigorous and conclusive test of worth or value

Example: The project's success will be determined by the results of the acid test.

acme /ɑkmi/

the highest point of achievement or excellence

Example: The athlete's acme was winning the Olympic gold medal.

acne /ɑkni/

a skin disease in which pus-filled spots form on the face

Example: Dermatologists recommend avoiding oily foods to help prevent acne.

acolyte /ɑkəˌlaɪt/

a follower or attendant

Example: The acolyte lit the candles.

a person who assists a priest

Example: The priest was delighted to have a dedicated and helpful acolyte.

acorn /eɪkɔrn/

the fruit of the oak tree, consisting of a smooth nut in a cuplike base

Example: I placed an acorn next to the window for the squirrel.

acoustics /ɑkustɪks/

the scientific study of sound

Example: Acousticians are well-versed in acoustics.

acquaintance /əˈkweɪntəns/

a person whom one knows slightly

Example: I ran into an old acquaintance at the grocery store yesterday.

acquisition /ɑkwəˈzɪʃən/

something acquired, often to add to a collection

Example: The museum's latest acquisition is one of Pablo's paintings.

acquittal /ɑkwɪtəl/

the judgement by a court that the accused is not guilty

Example: After a long trial, the jury delivered an acquittal.

acre /ˈeɪkɚ/

a unit of area equal to 4840 square yards

Example: My grandparents divided the acre of land among their children.

acrimony /ɑkrɪˌmoʊni/

bitterness and resentment felt about something

Example: There was a lot of acrimony between the two political parties.

acrobat /ɑkrəˌbɑt/

an entertainer who performs gymnastic feats requiring skill, agility, and balance

Example: The acrobat dazzled the audience with his impressive flips.

acronym /ɑkrənɪm/

a word made from the initial letters of other words

Example: This advertisement includes the acronym BOGO, Buy One, Get One.

acropolis /ɑkrɔpəlɪs/

the citadel of an ancient Greek city

Example: The Acropolis of Athens is a famous landmark in Greece.

acrylic acid /ɑkrɪlɪk, ɑsɪd/

a strong-smelling colourless corrosive liquid

Example: Manufacturers often add acrylic acid to latex paint to improve its water resistance and durability.

acrylic fibre /əˈkrɪlɪk, ˈfaɪbɚ/

a man-made fibre used for clothes and blankets

Example: My favourite sweater is made of soft acrylic fibre.

acrylic resin /ɑkrɪlɪk, ˈrɛzən/

any of a group of polymers of acrylic acid, used as synthetic rubbers, in paints, and as plastics

Example: The production of adhesives requires acrylic resin.

act /ɑkt/

something done

Example: Your act of kindness is truly remarkable.

a formal decision reached by a law-making body

Example: The act was passed with overwhelming support from both political parties.

a major division of a play

Example: The second act of Julius Caesar was the most suspenseful.

a pretended attitude

Example: Her friendly act was just a façade.

acting /ɑktɪŋ/

the art of an actor

Example: She pursues her career in acting.

action /ɑkʃən/

doing something for a particular purpose

Example: Your action puzzles me.

a lawsuit

Example: Mr. Jones will be taking legal action against his neighbour for the loud music.

activist /ɑktɪvəst/

a person who works energetically to achieve political or social goals

Example: The feminist activist organised a rally to raise awareness about gender inequality.

activity /ɑktˈɪvɪti/

the state of being active

Example: Regular physical activity is important for maintaining good health.

lively movement

Example: Their activity filled the air with laughter and energetic movement.

actor /ɑktɚ/

a male who acts in a play or film

Example: The actor played the role as Caius Cassius excellently.

actuality /ɑktʃuɑləˌti/

reality

Example: The report provides an overview of the current actuality of the global economy.

actuary /ɑktʃuˈɛri/

a person qualified to calculate commercial risks and probabilities involving uncertain future events

Example: The firm hired an actuary to determine the risk of investing in the stock market.

acuity /əkjuəti/

keenness of vision or thought

Example: The photographer has keen acuity for lighting and composition to capture striking images.

acumen /ɑkjumən/

the ability to make good decisions

Example: The CEO's business acumen helped her steer the company towards success.

acupuncture /ɑkjuˌpəŋktʃɚ/

a medical treatment involving the insertion of needles at various parts of the body to stimulate the nerve impulses

Example: Many people do not know acupuncture is an ancient traditional practice.

actress /ɑktrɛs/

a female who acts in a play or film

Example: The actress portrayed the character of Cleopatra.

ad /ɑd/

an advertisement

Example: This ad is annoying.

adage /ɑdədʒ/

a traditional saying that is generally accepted as being true

Example: My teacher reads an adage to the class every day.

adaptation /ɑdəpˈteɪʃən/

something that is produced by adapting something else

Example: The movie is an adaptation of the popular novel <u>Mississippi Masala.</u>

adaptor /ɑdɑptɚ/

a device used to connect several electrical appliances to a single socket

Example: I am unable to charge my phone because my adaptor is broken.

adder /ɑdɚ/

a small poisonous snake with a black zigzag pattern along the back

Example: I nearly stepped on an adder while hiking.

addict /ɑdɪkt/

a person who is unstable to stop taking narcotic drugs

Example: The addict steals money to purchase weed.

addiction /ɑdɪkʃən/

a sense of dependency

Example: I want to overcome my coffee addiction.

addition /ɑdˈɪʃən/

a mathematical operation in which the total of two or more numbers or quantities is calculated

Example: The addition of three and seven results in a sum of ten.

additive /ɑdətɪv/

any substance added to something to improve it or prevent deterioration

Example: The food company has an additive to the new recipe to enhance its flavour.

address /ɑdrˈɛs/

the place at which someone lives

Example: I have his new address.

a formal speech

Example: The president gave an address to the nation regarding the new tax policy.

addressee /ɑdrɛˈsi/

a person to whom a letter or parcel is addressed

Example: The addressee of the package was not at home.

adherent /ədˈhɛrənt/

a supporter or follower

Example: John was a strong adherent of the political party.

adhesion /ɑdˈhiʒən/

the quality or condition of sticking together

Example: The adhesion between the tape and the wall was strong.

adhesive /ɑdˈhisɪv/

a substance used for sticking things together

Example: I used adhesive to glue the broken vase.

adjective /ɑdʒɪktɪv/

a word that adds information about a noun or pronoun

Example: She uses an abundance of adjectives in her writing.

adjunct /ɑdʒəŋkt/

something added that is not essential

Example: The professor used a PowerPoint presentation as an adjunct to her lecture.

adjustment /əˈdʒəstmənt/

a slight alteration

Example: The mechanic made a quick adjustment to the car brakes.

adman /ɑdmən/

a man who works in advertising

Example: The adman came up with a clever campaign slogan.

administration /ədmɪnɪstrəʃən/

management of the affairs of an organisation

Example: The school administration tried in vain to reduce absenteeism.

a government

Example: The new administration prioritises improving infrastructure over health care.

administrator /ədˈmɪnəˌstreɪtə/

a person who administers an organisation

Example: The school administrator worked closely with parents and teachers.

admiral /ɑdmɪrɑl/

a naval officer of the highest rank

Example: The admiral surveyed the fleet before giving the order to set sail.

any of various brightly coloured butterflies

Example: I saw an admiral fluttering by in my garden this morning.

admission /ədˈmɪʃən/

permission or the right to enter

Example: The price of admission to the indigenous village includes access to all exhibits and a guided tour.

a confession

Example: The suspect's admission of guilt was the key piece of evidence that led to his conviction.

admittance /ədˈmɪtəns/

the act of entering a place with permission

Example: The usher checked the attendees' tickets before granting admittance to the theatre.

adolescence /ˌadəˈlɛsəns/

the period between puberty and adulthood

Example: During adolescence, most teenagers undergo significant physical, emotional, and cognitive changes.

adoption /ɑdɑpʃən/

the act of making legally one's own

Example: The couple went through a rigorous process to finalise the adoption of their new daughter.

adrenaline /ɑdrɛnələn/

a hormone secreted by the adrenal gland in response to stress

Example: I felt a sudden rush of adrenaline after I heard of the accident.

adult /ɑdʌlt/

a mature fully grown person, animal, or plant

Example: In most countries, a person is considered an adult when they reach the age of 18.

adulthood /ɑdˈʌlthʊd/

a fully grown or matured person, animal, or plant

Example: During adulthood, individuals usually support themselves financially.

advancement /ɑdˈvænsmənt/

promotion in rank or status

Example: Mary's advancement to a managerial position is due to nepotism.

advantage /ɑdvˈæntɪdʒ/

a more favourable position

Example: Having a flexible schedule can be a significant advantage for working people.

advent /ɑdˌvɛnt/

an arrival

Example: The advent of digital technology has revolutionised the way we communicate.

the season that includes the four Sundays before Christmas

Example: Advent is a time of reflection, preparation, and hope.

Adventist /ɑdˌvɛntɪst/

a member of a Christian group that believes in the imminent return of Christ

Example: Jemma is an Adventist and wants the administrators to postpone the game to accommodate her.

adventure /ɑdˈvɛntʃɚ/

a risky undertaking, the ending of which is uncertain

Example: Going to the safari in Africa can be an incredible adventure.

exciting or unexpected events

Example: Sometimes the best adventure is the unexpected one that comes our way.

adventurer /ɑdˈvɛntʃrə/

a person who seeks money or power by unscrupulous means

Example: The adventurer swindled his way to the top of the company.

a person who seeks adventure

Example: The adventurer set out on a solo trek across the Himalayas.

adverb /ɑdvʌrb/

a word that modifies a sentence, verb, adverb, or adjective.

Example: The teacher asked the students to use an adverb in the sentence.

adversary /ɑdvɚˌsɛri/

an opponent in a fight, disagreement, or sporting contest

Example: In the boxing match, Tyson's adversary was a tough opponent.

adversity /ad'vʌrsɪˌti/

very hard or difficult circumstances

Example: Facing bankruptcy and unemployment was a great adversity for her.

advertisement /advɝ'tɪzmənt/

any public announcement designed to sell goods or publicize an event

Example: This advertisement is quite appealing.

advertorial /advɝ'tɔriəl/

advertising presented as if it is editorial material

Example: The magazine published a controversial advertorial in their latest issue.

advertising /advɚtˌaɪzɪŋ/

the activity or profession of producing advertisements for commercial services

Example: Advertising is an essential part of marketing.

advice /adv'aɪs/

recommendation as to an appropriate choice of action

Example: I need your advice on what kind of investment to make.

advocacy /advəkəsi/

native support of a cause or course of action

Example: Advocacy includes public speaking and lobbying to social media campaigns and community organizing.

aegis /'idʒəs/

with the sponsorship or protection of

Example: This project is conducted under the aegis of the government.

aerial /ariəl/

the metal pole or wire on a television or radio which transmits or receive signals

Example: I adjusted the aerial on my television to get better reception.

acrobatics /ˌakrəˈbɑtɪks/

spectacular manoeuvres performed by acrobats.

Example: The gymnasts amazed the audience with their acrobatics.

aerobics /ɑrobɪks/

exercises to increase the amount of oxygen in the blood and strengthen the heart and lungs

Example: Aerobics is a popular form of exercise.

aerodrome /ˈɑrəˌdroʊm/

a small airport

Example: The small town had only one aerodrome for its residents.

aerosol /ˈɛrəˌsɔl/

a small metal pressurized can from which a substance can be dispensed in a fine spray

Example: I sprayed the weeds in the garden using an aerosol pesticide.

aerospace /ˈɛroʊspeɪs/

the earth's atmosphere and space beyond

Example: This organisation specialises in the exploration of aerospace.

aesthetics /ɛsˈθɛtɪks/

the branch of philosophy concerned with the study of the concepts of beauty and taste

Example: Many people appreciate the aesthetics of modern art.

affair /afˈɛr/

an event or happening

Example: The charity event was the biggest affair of the year.

something previously specified

Example: The affair I want to discuss with you is of utmost importance.

an extramarital relationship

Example: She had an affair with her boss.

affectation /afɛkteʃən/

an attitude or manner put on to impress others

Example: She spoke in a British accent with an affectation to impress her new friends.

affection afɛkʃən/

fondness or tenderness for a person or thing

Example: She felt great affection for her grandmother.

affidavit /ˌafədeɪvɪt/

a written statement made under oath

Example: The lawyer submitted an affidavit to the court.

affinity /afɪnəti/

a feeling of closeness to and understanding of a person

Example: She felt an affinity for her new co-worker.

a close similarity in appearance, structure, or quality

Example: There is an affinity between the two languages.

affliction /aflɪkʃən/

something that cause physical or mental suffering

Example: His chronic back pain was a constant affliction that limited his mobility and quality of life.

affront /əˈfrənt/

a deliberate insult hurting someone's pride or dignity

Example: He took my comments as a personal affront and became quite angry with me.

after-birth /aftɚ, ˈbɚθ/

the placenta and foetal membranes expelled from the mother's womb after childbirth

Example: After the baby was born, the doctor checked to make sure the after-birth was delivered.

after-care /ɑftɚ, ˈkɛr/

the help or support given to a person discharged from a hospital or prison

Example: After undergoing surgery, the patient received excellent after-care from the hospital staff.

after-damp /ɑftɚ, ˈdɑmp/

a poisonous gas formed after the explosion of firedamp in a coal mine

Example: Several miners were affected by the deadly after-damp.

after-effect /ɑftər, ˈifɛkt/

any result occurring sometime after its caused

Example: The earthquake had many after-effects, including power outages and a shortage of drinking water.

after-glow /ɑftɚ, ˈglo/

the glow left after the source of a light has disappeared

Example: We enjoyed the peaceful after-glow that lingered in the sky after sunset.

after-life /ɑftɚ, laɪf/

life after death

Example: Many people believe in an after-life.

aftermath /ɑftərˌmæθ/

effects or results of an event considered collectively

Example: The aftermath of the hurricane was devastating.

afternoon /ˌæftərˈnun/

the period between noon and evening

Example: This afternoon is peaceful.

after-pain /ɑftɚ, ˈpeɪn/ /

pain caused by contraction of a woman's womb after childbirth

Example: The mother experienced severe after-pain following the delivery of her triplet.

aftershave /ɑftəˈʃeɪv/

a scented lotion applied to a man's face after shaving

Example: He always applies aftershave to keep his skin smooth.

aftershock /ɑftəˌʃɒk/

one of a series of minor tremors occurring after the main shock of an earthquake

Example: The aftershock of the earthquake was felt throughout the region for several weeks.

afterthought /ˈɑftɚ, ˈθɔt/

something thought of after the opportunity to use it has passed

Example: I realized as an afterthought that I should have brought my umbrella with me.

an addition to something already completed

Example: The afterthought of adding a new paragraph made the essay more comprehensive.

agar /ˈeɪgɚ/

a jelly-like substance obtained from seaweed and used as a thickener in food

Example: Agar is often used in microbiology to cultivate bacteria.

agate /ˈægət/

a hard semiprecious form of quartz with striped colouring

Example: He gave his girlfriend a beautiful necklace made of agate.

age /ˈeɪdʒ/

the length of time that a person or thing has existed

Example: He is quite grown for his age.

agency /ˈeɪdʒənsi/

an organization providing a specific service

Example: I am looking for a model agency.

agenda /ədʒɛndə/

a schedule or list of items to be attended to

Example: The speaker outlined the agenda for the audience.

agent /ˈeɪdʒənt/

a person who arranges business for other people

Example: The real estate agent helped us find the perfect house for our family.

a substance which causes change in other substances

Example: The cleaning agent removed the stubborn stains from the carpet.

agglomeration /əglʌməreʃən/

a confused mass or cluster

Example: The agglomeration of cars on the highway caused a major traffic jam.

aggregate /ɑgrəgeɪt/

an amount or total formed from separate units

Example: The aggregate of all the small donations amounted to a significant contribution to the charity.

a rock consisting of a mixture of minerals

Example: This concrete is made of fine aggregate and coarse aggregate mixed with cement and water.

aggression /əˈgrɛʃən/

violent and hostile behaviour

Example: My country condemned the aggression of the neighbouring country.

agitprop /ˈædʒətˌprɔp/

political agitation and propaganda

Example: During the Cold War, agitprop was commonly used to influence public opinion in favour of their respective ideologies.

agnostic /ægˈnɑstɪk/

a person who believes that it is impossible to know whether God exists

Example: Even though I was raised in a religious household, I became more of an agnostic and questioned the existence of God.

a person who claims that the answers to some specific questions cannot be known with certainty

Example: The scientist was agnostic about the cause of the anomaly and sought further evidence to explain it.

agony /ɑgəni/

acute physical or mental pain

Example: The patient was writhing in agony due to the severe burn on his arm.

agoraphobia /əˌgɔrəˈfoʊbiə/

a pathological fear of being in public places

Example: Sarah's agoraphobia prevented her from leaving her house for weeks at a time.

agreement /ɑgriːmənt/

the act of agreeing

Example: The two parties came to an agreement about the terms of their partnership.

a legally enforceable contract

Example: They signed a rental agreement before moving into the apartment.

agriculture /ɑgrɪˌkəltʃə/

the rearing of crops and livestock; farming

Example: John comes from a long line of farmers and is passionate about agriculture.

agrochemical /ˌɑgroˈkɛmɪkəl/

a chemical used in agriculture

Example: Farmers often use agrochemicals to protect their crops from pests, weeds, and diseases.

agronomy /əˈgrɑnəˌmi/

the science of land cultivation, soil management, and crop production

Example: Agronomy is a critical field of study for farmers and agricultural professionals.

aid /ˈeɪd/

money, equipment, or services provided for people in need

Example: International organisations rallied together to provide aid to the affected region.

aide /ˈeɪd/

an assistant

Example: The CEO's aide efficiently managed her busy schedule.

aileron /ˈeɪlɚˌɑn/

a hinged flap on the back of an aircraft wing which controls rolling

Example: The aileron on the wing of the airplane responded to the pilot's input.

ailment /ˈeɪlmənt/

a slight illness

Example: Thankfully, her ailment was short-lived.

air /ˈɛr/

the mixture of gases that forms the earth's atmosphere

Example: The climbers took deep breaths of the crisp mountain air as they reached the summit.

airbrush /ˈɛrˌbrəʃ/

an atomizer which sprays paint by means of compressed air

Example: The artist dexterously used an airbrush to create stunning gradients and fine details in their painting.

air commodore /ˈer, ˈkʌməˌdɔr/

a senior officer in an air force

Example: As an air commodore, Alex oversaw the successful implementation of advanced aerial tactics and training programs.

aircraft /ˈɛrkræft/

any machine capable of flying

Example: The aviation museum displayed one blue aircraft.

aircushion /ˈɛr, ˈkʊʃən/

an inflatable cushion

Example: The aircushion provided a comfortable seating option during the outdoor concert.

the pocket of air that supports a hovercraft

Example: The pilot adjusted the air cushion to control the height and stability of the hovercraft during navigation.

airfield /ˈɛrˌfild/

a place where aircrafts can land and take off

Example: The small town built an airfield to attract aviation enthusiasts.

air-force /ˈɛrfɔrs/

the branch of a nation's armed services that is responsible of air welfare

Example: The air-force conducted a series of strategic airstrikes to weaken the enemy's defences.

airing /ˈɛrɪŋ/

exposure to air or warmth for drying or ventilation

Example: After washing the clothes, I hung them on the clothesline for airing and drying.

exposure to public debate

Example: The politician agreed to appear on the talk show for an airing of his views on the controversial topic.

airlift /'ɛrˌlɪft/

the transportation by air of troops or cargo when other routes are blocked

Example: The military conducted an airlift to deploy troops and supplies to a remote military base.

airline /'ɛrlaɪn/

an organization that provides scheduled flights for passengers or cargo

Example: I booked a ticket with a reputable airline for my upcoming trip to Europe.

airlock /'ɛrˌlɔk/

a bubble of air blocking the flow of liquid in a pipe

Example: The plumber used a specialised tool to clear the airlock and restore the water flow.

airmail /'ɛrˌmeɪl/

the system of sending mail by aircraft

Example: I sent the important documents via airmail.

air-pocket /'ɛr, 'pʌkət/

a small descending air current that causes an aircraft to lose height suddenly

Example: As the airplane flew through the stormy weather, it hit an unexpected air pocket.

airport /'ɛrpoːrt/

a landing and taking-off area for civil aircraft

Example: The airport was temporarily closed due to heavy fog.

air-pressure /'ɛr, 'prɛʃɚ/

the force exerted on the earth by the air

Example: As the storm approached, the air-pressure dropped rapidly.

air pump /ˈɛr, ˈpʌmp/

a device used for pumping air into or out of something

Example: I used an air pump to inflate the bicycle tires before going for a ride.

air raid /ˈɛr, ˈreɪd/

an attack by enemy aircraft in which bombs are dropped

Example: Some historical sites still bear the scars of the air raid that took place during the conflict.

air resistance /ˈɛr, rɪˈzɪstəns/

the force produced by the air when an object is moving through it

Example: The streamlined design of a racing car minimises air resistance.

airs /ˈɛrz/

manners put on to impress people

Example: At the formal dinner, John put on his best airs.

air ship /ˈɛr, ˈʃɪp/

a lighter-than-air self-propelled aircraft

Example: The air ship gracefully floated above the city.

air side /ˈɛr, ˈsaɪd/

the part of an airport nearest the aircraft

Example: Access to the air side of the airport is restricted to authorized personnel only.

airspace /ˈɛrspeɪs/

the atmosphere above a particular country, regarded as its territory

Example: The military aircraft entered the country's airspace without authorisation.

airspeed /ˈɛrspiːd/

the speed of an aircraft relative to the air in which it moves

Example: The pilot relied on the accurate measurement of airspeed to calculate the estimated time of arrival.

airstrip /ˈɛrstrɪp/

a cleared area for the landing and taking-off of aircraft

Example: Lethem has a narrow airstrip.

airtime /ˈɛrtaɪm/

the time allocated to a particular programme, topic, or type of material on radio or television

Example: The news anchor used limited airtime to deliver relevant updates.

airwaves /ˈɛrweɪvz/

radio waves used in radio and television broadcasting

Example: Television programmes are broadcasted over the airwaves.

airway /ˈɛrweɪ/

an air route used regularly by aircraft

Example: The transatlantic airway is a vital route used regularly by aircraft.

aisle /aɪəl/

a passageway separating seating areas in a church, theatre, or cinema, or separating rows of shelves in a supermarket

Example: People walked down the narrow aisle of the church.

aitchbone /ˈeɪtʃboʊn/

a cut of beef from the rump bone

Example: The butcher displayed a fresh aitchbone in the meat section.

alabaster /ˌɑləbˈæstɚ/

a kind of white stone used for making statues and vases

Example: The sculptor meticulously carved a delicate figure out of smooth alabaster.

alacrity /alakrɪti/

speed or eagerness

Example: With great alacrity, she responded to the opportunity, eager to seize the moment.

alarm /alˈɑːrm/

fear aroused by awareness of danger

Example: Her heart raced with alarm as she heard a loud crash coming from downstairs.

alarmist /alˈɑːrmɪst/

a person who alarms others needlessly

Example: The news article was criticised for its alarmist tone, needlessly instilling fear and panic in readers.

albacore /albɐkˌoːr/

a tuna found in warm seas which is valued as a food fish

Example: The fisherman reeled in a large albacore during their deep-sea fishing expedition.

albatross /albəˌtrɔs/

a large sea bird with very long wings

Example: The majestic albatross gracefully glided above the ocean.

albino /alˈbaɪˌno/

a person or animal with white or almost white hair and skin and pinkish eyes

Example: The albino fascinated the crowd with his unique appearance.

album /ˈalbʌm/

a book with blank pages, for keeping photographs or stamps in

Example: I cherish the memories captured in my photo album.

a long-playing CD or record

Example: Taylor's latest album is phenomenal.

alchemy /ɑlkəmi/

a medieval form of chemistry concerned with trying to change base metals into gold and to find an elixir to prolong life indefinitely

Example: Alchemy captivated the minds of many scholars.

alcohol /ˈɑlkəˌɔːl/

a colourless flammable liquid present in intoxicating drinks

Example: The doctor advised the patient to avoid consuming alcohol.

alcoholic /ɑlkəˈhɔlɪk/

a person who is addicted to alcohol

Example: The alcoholic sought treatment to overcome his addiction.

alcoholism /ɑlkəˌhɔˌlɪzəm/

a condition in which dependence on alcohol harms a person's health and everyday life

Example: Alcoholism can lead to severe health complications.

alcove /ɑlˌkoʊv/

a recess in the wall of a room

Example: The alcove in the hallway was adorned with a beautiful piece of artwork.

alder /ˈɔldɚ/

a tree with toothed leaves and cone-like fruits, often found in damp places

Example: The graceful silhouette of the alder caught my attention.

alderman /ˈɔldɚmən/

a senior member of a local council, elected by other councillors

Example: The alderman proposed a new initiative to improve community infrastructure.

ale /ˈeɪl/

a beer fermented in an open vessel using yeast that rise to the top of the brew

Example: *I prefer to drink ale over lager.*

alfalfa /ˌalˈfælfə/

a plant widely used for feeding farm animals

Example: *The dairy farmer harvested bales of alfalfa to feed the cows.*

algae /ˈɑldʒi/

plants which grow in water or moist ground

Example: *The biologist studied the different species of algae present in the coastal ecosystem.*

algebra /ɑldʒəbrə/

a branch of mathematics in which symbols are used to represent numbers

Example: *Many students dislike algebra.*

algorithm /ˈɑlgɚ-rɪðəm/

a logical arithmetical or computational procedure for solving problems

Example: *The facial recognition software employs an algorithm to compare and match facial features.*

alibi /ɑləˌbaɪ/

a plea for being somewhere else when a crime was committed

Example: *The suspect claimed to have a solid alibi.*

alien /ˈeɪliən/

a person who is a citizen of a country other than the one in which he or she lives

Example: *The immigration officer interviewed the alien to determine her eligibility for a visa.*

alimony /ˈɑləˌmʌni/

an allowance paid under a court order by one spouse to another after separation

Example: *After their divorce, Alan was ordered by the court to pay alimony to his ex-wife.*

alkali /ɑlkəlaɪ/

a substance that combines with acid and neutralizes it to form a salt

Example: Adding a small amount of alkali to the solution helped to balance its acidity.

alkaloid /ˈɑlkəˌlɔɪd/

any of a group of organic compounds containing nitrogen

Example: The alkaloid found in this plant has potent medicinal properties.

alkene /ɑlkin/

any unsaturated hydrocarbon with the general formula C_nH_{2n}

Example: Pyrolysis gasoline contains a high amount of alkene.

allegation /ˌɑləˈgeɪʃən/

an unproved assertion or accusation

Example: I advise you to withdraw your allegation before I contact my lawyer.

allegiance /ɑlidʒəns/

loyalty or dedication to a person, cause, or belief

Example: He pledged his allegiance to the party.

allegory /ɑləˌgɔri/

a story, poem, or picture with an underlying meaning as well as a literal one

Example: Students were asked to identify the main allegory in the poem.

allele /əˈlɛli/

any of two or more genes that are responsible for alternative characteristics, such as smooth or wrinkled seeds in peas

Example: The allele for green eyes is dominant.

allergen /ɑlɚdʒən/

a substance capable of causing an allergic reaction

Example: Pollen is a common allergen for many people.

allergy /alɝdʒi/

extreme sensitivity to a substance which causes the body to react to any contact with it

Example: I have an allergy to flowers.

alley /ali/

a narrow passage between or behind buildings

Example: The detective followed the suspect into a dark alley behind the buildings.

a path in a garden, often lined with trees

Example: They discovered a charming alley in the park, adorned with blooming flowers and benches.

alliance /əˈlaɪəns/

the state of being allied

Example: The two companies formed an alliance to develop a new technology product.

a formal relationship between two or more countries or political parties to work together

Example: The alliance between the countries led to increased trade and cooperation in various fields.

alligator /aləˌgeɪtɝ/

a large reptile of the southern US, like the crocodile but with a shorter broader snout

Example: There was an alligator in the pond.

alliteration /alıtəreıʃən/

the use of the same sound at the start of words occurring together

Example: The poet used a brilliant alliteration to create a musical effect.

allotment /alɔstmənt/

a small piece of land rented by a person to grow vegetables on

Example: The allotment was made on Wednesday.

allotrope /alə‚trop/

any of two or more physical forms in which an element can exist

Example: This crystalline allotrope is grey.

allowance /alaʊəns/

an amount or money given at regular intervals

Example: My mother gives me a weekly allowance.

alloy /alɔɪ/

a mixture of two or more metals

Example: Brass is an alloy of copper and zinc.

allspice /ˈɔlspaɪs/

a spice used in cooking, which comes from the berries of an American tropical tree

Example: Our chef loves using allspice when preparing meals.

allure /əlʊr/

attractiveness or appeal

Example: The allure of foreign bonds is obvious.

allusion /əˈluʒən/

an indirect reference

Example: The allusion to Cinderella was brilliant.

ally /ali/

a country, person, or group with an agreement to support each other

Example: He found a strong ally in his colleague.

alma mater /ˈalmə ˈmætər/

the school, college, or university that one attended

Example: He offered scholarships to top-performing students of his alma mater.

almanac /ˈɑlməˌnæk/

a yearly calendar with detailed information on matters like anniversaries and phases of the moon

Example: This almanac has beautiful artworks.

almond /ˈɑmənd/

an edible oval nut with a yellowish-brown shell, which grows on a small tree

Example: She grated an almond and sprinkled it on top of the salad.

almoner /ˈɑlmənər/

a former name for a hospital social worker

Example: The almoner worked closely with patients and their families.

alms /ˈɑlmz/

donations of money or goods to the poor

Example: The church organised a charity drive to collect alms for the less fortunate.

alms-house /ˈɑlmz, ˈhaʊs/

a house, financed by charity, which offered accommodation to the poor

Example: The local community raised funds to build an alms-house.

aloe /ɑlo/

a plant with fleshy spiny leaves

Example: The aloe in the garden bloomed with vibrant flowers.

aloe vera /ɑlo, ˈvɛrə/

a plant producing a juice which is used to treat skin and hair

Example: Many people rely on the cooling and healing properties of aloe vera to alleviate sunburns.

alpaca /ɑlpækə/

a South American mammal related to the llama, with dark shaggy hair

Example: My pet is an alpaca.

alpha /ɑlfə/

the first letter in the Greek alphabet

Example: Alpha is used as a mathematical symbol.

the highest grade in an examination or for a piece of academic work

Example: Receiving an alpha on the final exam was a testament to the student's exceptional understanding of the subject matter.

alphabet /ɑlfəˌbɛt/

a set of letters in fixed conventional order, used in a writing system

Example: Most children are taught the alphabet at home.

altar /'ɔltɚ/

the table used for Communion in Christian churches

Example: The priest stood at the altar, leading the congregation in prayers.

a raised structure on which sacrifices are offered and religious rites performed

Example: The people gathered around the stone altar to participate in the sacred rites and make offerings to their deity.

altarpiece /'ɔltɚ, 'pis/

a painting or a decorated screen set above and behind the altar in a Christian church

Example: The altarpiece was commissioned from a renowned artist.

alteration /ɑltɚ'eɪʃən/

a change or modification

Example: After trying on the uniform, she requested an alteration.

altercation /ˌɔltɚ'keɪʃən/

a noisy argument

Example: The politician's controversial statement sparked an altercation during the public debate.

alternative /ɔltɚnətɪv/

a possibility of choice between two or more things

Example: The company explored an alternative for reducing costs without having to lay off employees.

alternator /ˈɔltɚˌneɪtɚ/

an electrical machine that generates an alternating current

Example: The car's alternator provides electrical power to charge the battery.

altimeter /alˈtɪmətɚ/

an instrument that measures altitude

Example: Hikers often carry an altimeter to track their elevation.

altitude /ɔltəˌtud/

height, especially above sea level

Example: We were flying at an altitude above 50,000 feet.

altruism /ɔltruˌɪzəm/

unselfish concern for the welfare of others

Example: She was torn between altruism and self-interest.

alum /aləm/

a double sulphate of aluminium and potassium, used in manufacturing and in medicine

Example: Many stores sell alum.

aluminium /aljumɪnəm/

a light malleable silvery-white metallic element that does not rust

Example: Aluminium is a conductive metal.

alumni /alˈʌmni/

a body of graduates of a school, college, or university

Example: Several alumni agreed to raise funds for the school.

alumnus /alˈʌmnʌs/

a graduate of a school, college, or university

Example: My father is an alumnus of The University of the West Indies.

alyssum /ɑlɪsəm/

a garden plant with clusters of small white flowers

Example: She planted alyssum along the border of her garden.

amateur /aməˌtʃʌr/

a person who engages in a sport or other activity as a pastime rather than as a profession

Example: She is an amateur in photography.

ambassador /ɑmˈbæsədə/

a diplomat of the highest rank, sent to another country as permanent representative of his or her own country

Example: Aiden is an ambassador to Guyana.

amber /ɑmbər/

a yellow translucent fossilised resin used in jewellery

Example: The artisan crafted a unique pendant using a large piece of amber.

ambergris /ɑmbərgrɪs/

a waxy substance secreted by the sperm whale, which is used in making perfume

Example: Perfume makers use ambergris as a fixative in their creations.

ambience /ɑmbiəns/

the atmosphere of a place

Example: The restaurant has a pleasant ambience.

ambiguity /ɑmbɪgˈjuɪti/

the possibility of interpreting an expression in more than one way

Example: The novel's ending was intentionally crafted with ambiguity.

ambition /amb'ɪʃən/

strong desire for success

Example: His ambition drove him to work tirelessly and pursue his dream of becoming a successful entrepreneur.

a goal

Example: His ambition was to climb Mount Everest.

ambivalence /am'bɪvələns/

the state of feeling two conflicting emotions at the same time

Example: Katy was certain about her moral ambivalence.

ambulance /ambjʊləns/

a motor vehicle designed to carry sick or injured people

Example: We called for an ambulance immediately.

ambush /amˌbʊʃ/

the act of waiting in a concealed position to make a surprise attack

Example: A soldier has been shot in an ambush.

amendment /ə'mɛndmənt/

an improvement or correction

Example: A major amendment was added to the tax laws.

Americanism /amɛrɪkəˌnɪzəm/

an expression or custom that is characteristic of the people of the United States of America

Example: I recognised the Americanism as she dipped into her handbag.

amino acid /əmino,'æsɪd/

any of a group of organic compounds containing the amino group, $-NH_2$, and one or more carboxyl groups, $-COOH$, especially one that is a compound of protein

Example: Glycine is the simplest amino acid.

ammeter /ɑmitər/
an instrument for measuring an electric current in amperes
Example: The students were very attentive to the ammeter.

ammonia /ɑmonjə/
a colourless strong-smelling gas containing hydrogen and nitrogen
Example: Ammonia has a very pungent scent.

amnesia /ɑmˈniʒə/
a partial or total loss of memory
Example: Amnesia can be caused by emotional trauma.

amnesty /ɑmnəsti/
a general pardon for offences against a government
Example: Many political prisons are freed under an amnesty.

amniotic fluid /ɑmniɔtɪk, ˈfluɪd/
the fluid surrounding the foetus in the womb
Example: Amniotic fluid acts as a lubricant during labour.

amoeba /əˈmibə/
a microscopic single-cell creature that can change its shape
Example: Amoeba is a unicellular organism.

amount /ɑmˈaʊnt/
extent or quantity
Example: Alice made a considerable amount of money in her recent business.

amour /ˌɑˈmur/
a secret love affair
Example: He engaged in a passionate amour with a married woman.

amperage /ɑmˌpərɪdʒ/

the strength of an electric current measured in amperes

Example: The circuit breaker is designed to handle a maximum amperage of 20 amps.

ampere /ɑmˌpər/

the basic unit of electric current

Example: The electronic device draws a current of 2 amperes.

amphibian /ɑmˈfɪbiən/

animals, such as a newt, frog, or toad that lives on land but breeds in water

Example: Amphibian is an important species in the ecosystem.

amplifier /ɑmpləˌfaɪər/

an electronic device used to increase the strength of a current or sound signal

Example: The guitarist plugged his instrument into the amplifier.

amplitude /ɑmpləˌtud/

greatness of extent

Example: The amplitude of the seismic waves was so great that it caused significant damage to buildings in the affected area.

amputee /ɑmpjəˈti/

a person who has had a limb amputated

Example: Her life as an amputee is challenging.

amulet /ɑmjʊlɛt/

a trinket or jewel worn as a protection against evil

Example: She wore an amulet around her neck.

amusement /əmˈjuzmənt/

the state of being amused

Example: His eyes sparked with amusement.

anaconda /ɑnəˈkɔndə/

a large South American snake which squeezes its prey to death

Example: The largest anaconda is reportedly in South America.

anaerobe /ɑnərˌoʊb/

an organism that does not require oxygen

Example: Yeast is an anaerobe.

anagram /ɑnəˌgræm/

a word or phrase made by rearranging the letters of another word or phrase

Example: The word "listen" can be rearranged to form the anagram "silent."

analgesia /ɑnɐld͡ʒˈiːʒə/

the absence of pain

Example: The doctor administered a local anaesthetic to provide analgesia and numb the area.

analgesic /ɑnɐld͡ʒˈiːzɪk/

a drug that relieves pain

Example: She took an analgesic to alleviate the headache.

analogue /ɑnəlˌɔg/

a physical object or quantity used to measure or represent another quantity

Example: The thermometer is an analogue device that uses the expansion of liquid to indicate temperature.

analysis /ɑnˈɑləsˌɪs/

the separation of a whole into parts for study or interpretation; statement of the results of this

Example: All students are required to write an analysis of the poems studied.

analyst /ˈɑnɐlˌɪst/

a person who is skilled in analysis

Example: I want to be a financial analyst.

anarchy /ɑnərˌki/

general lawlessness and disorder

Example: Many countries in the world are in a perpetual state of anarchy.

anatomist /əˈnɑtəməst/

an expert in anatomy

Example: The anatomist carefully dissected the cadaver to study the intricate details.

anatomy /əˈnɑtəmi/

the science of the physical structure of animals and plants

Example: Students spend a significant amount of time studying anatomy to understand the complexities of the human body.

ancestor /ɑnˌsɛstə/

a person in former times from whom one is descended

Example: She worshipped her ancestors.

ancestry /ɑnsɛstri/

family descent

Example: He delved into his genealogy and traced his ancestry back to several different countries.

anchor /ɑŋkə/

a hooked device attached to a boat by a cable and dropped overboard to fasten the boat to the sea bottom

Example: The sailor threw the anchor overboard to stabilise the boat.

anchorage /ˈɑŋkərədʒ/

a place where a boat can be anchored

Example: The yacht found a calm and sheltered anchorage in the bay.

anchorite /ˈɑŋkərˌaɪt/

a person who chooses to live in isolation for religious reasons

Example: The anchorite devoted their life to prayer and meditation.

anchovy /ˈɑnˌtʃovi/

a small marine food fish with a salty taste

Example: I only ordered one slice of pizza with anchovy on it.

android /ˈɑnˌdrɔɪd/

a robot resembling a human being

Example: The advanced android was designed to perform human-like tasks.

andrology /ɑndrˈɑːlədʒi/

the branch of medicine concerned with diseases and conditions specific to men

Example: Brandon is specialised in andrology.

anecdote /ˈɑnəkˌdot/

a short amusing account of an incident

Example: Uncle Tom entertained everyone with a humorous anecdote from his childhood.

anaemia /əˈnimiə/

a deficiency of red blood cells or their haemoglobin content, resulting in a paleness and lack of energy

Example: The patient's persistent anaemia was treated with iron supplements.

anemometer /ˌɑnəˈmʌmətɚ/

an instrument for recording wind speed

Example: The meteorologist used an anemometer to measure the wind speed.

anaesthesia /ˌanɪsˈθiʒə/

loss of bodily feeling caused by disease or accident or by drugs such as ether

Example: The anaesthesiologist administered the anaesthesia to the patient before the surgery.

anaesthetic /ˌanəsˈθɛtɪk/

a substance that causes anaesthesia

Example: The dentist administered the anaesthetic to numb the patient's mouth before the dental procedure.

anaesthetist /əˈnɛsθətəst/

a doctor who administers anaesthetic

Example: The anaesthetist carefully monitored the patient's vital signs.

angel /ˈeɪndʒəl/

a spiritual being believed to be an attendant or messenger of God

Example: Lucifer was an angel.

anger /ˈɑŋɡər/

a feeling of extreme annoyance or displeasure

Example: His face turned red with anger as he shouted at the rude driver.

angina /ɑnˈdʒaɪnə/

a sudden intense pain in the chest caused by a momentary lack of adequate blood supply to the heart muscle

Example: The patient experienced angina and sought immediate medical attention.

angle /ˈɑŋɡəl/

the space between or shape formed by two straight lines or surfaces that meet

Example: She measured the angle between the two walls.

angst /ˈɑŋkst/

a feeling of anxiety

Example: He experienced a sense of angst and uncertainty.

anguish /ˈaŋgwɪʃ/

great mental pain

Example: The mother's heart was filled with anguish as she waited for news about her missing child.

animal /ˈanɪməl/

any living being that is capable of voluntary movement and possesses specialized sense organs

Example: A domesticated cat is a friendly animal.

a cruel person

Example: He behaves like an animal.

animator /ˈanəˌmeɪtər/

a person who makes interesting and lively cartoons

Example: The talented animator brought the characters to life with vibrant colours and smooth movements.

ankle /ˈaŋkəl/

the joint connecting the leg and the foot

Example: She twisted her ankle while running.

anklet /ˈaŋklɛt/

an ornamental chain worn around the ankle

Example: She wore a delicate silver anklet with tiny charms that jingled softly.

anniversary /ˌanəˈvɜːsɚi/

the date on which an event occurred in some previous year

Example: They celebrated their 10th wedding anniversary with a romantic dinner.

announcer /əˈnaʊnsɚ/

a person who introduces programs on radio or television

Example: The sports announcer provided live commentary.

annuity /ɑnuəti/

a fixed sum payable at specific intervals over a period

Example: He decided to invest in an annuity to secure a steady income stream.

answer /ˈɑnsɚ/

a reply to a question, request, letter, or article

Example: She received a prompt and detailed answer to her inquiry.

a solution to a problem

Example: After hours of research, she finally found the answer to the challenging puzzle.

antagonism /ɑnˈtɑgəˌnɪzəm/

openly expressed hostility

Example: There was a strong antagonism between the two rival gangs.

antagonist /ɑnˈtɑgənəst/

an opponent or adversary

Example: In the novella, the hero's main antagonist was a cunning and powerful villain.

antecedent /ˌɑnˈtɛsədənt/

an event or circumstance that happens or exists before another

Example: The economic recession was the antecedent to widespread unemployment and social unrest.

a word or phrase to which a relative pronoun refers

Example: The antecedent is a critical component of pronoun usage in grammar.

anthem /ˈɑnθəm/

a song of loyalty or devotion

Example: The national anthem played as the flag was raised.

anther /ˈɑnθɚ/

the part of the stamen of a flower which contains the pollen

Example: In botany, the anther plays a vital role in the process of pollination.

anthrax /ˈanθræks/

a dangerous infectious disease of cattle and sheep

Example: The outbreak of anthrax among livestock led to significant economic losses.

antibiotic /ˌantaɪbaɪˈɒtɪk/

a chemical substance capable of destroying bacteria

Example: The doctor prescribed antibiotic for the bacterial infections.

antibody /ˈantiˌbɒdi/

a protein produced in the blood which destroys bacteria

Example: An antibody typically binds to antigens, recognising and binding to specific target molecules.

anticipation /anˌtɪsəˈpeɪʃən/

the act of anticipating

Example: The children waited in anticipation for their parents to arrive home with a surprise.

antidote /ˈantiˌdot/

a substance that counteracts a poison or harmful condition

Example: In case of snakebite, it is important to administer the appropriate antidote immediately.

antifreeze /ˈantiˌfriz/

a liquid added to water to lower its freezing point, used in the radiator of a motor vehicle to prevent freezing

Example: During winter, it is essential to use antifreeze in the car's cooling system.

antigen /ˈantədʒən/

a substance that causes the body to produce antibodies

Example: The antigen is a foreign substance that triggers an immune response in the body.

anxiety /aŋzˈaɪəti/

a state of uneasiness about what may happen

Example: She experienced anxiety before the job interview.

eagerness

Example: The children waited in anxiety for the announcement of the exam results.

apartment /apˈɑːrtmənt/

any room in a building, usually one of several forming a suite, used as a living accommodation

Example: My apartment is small and cosy.

apathy /ˈapəθi/

lack of interest or enthusiasm

Example: The employees' apathy towards their work resulted in decreased productivity.

aperture /ˈapərtʃər/

an opening in a camera or telescope that controls the amount of light entering it

Example: By adjusting the aperture of the camera, you can control the depth of field.

apex /ˈeɪˌpɛks/

the highest point

Example: The mountain climber reached the apex of the peak.

aphasia /əˈfeɪʒə/

a disorder of the central nervous system that affects the ability to use and understand words

Example: After the stroke, the patient experienced aphasia and had difficulty expressing her thoughts.

aphorism /ˈafɚˌɪzəm/

a short clever saying expressing a general truth

Example: One famous aphorism states, "Know thyself," emphasising the importance of self-awareness.

apiary /ˈeɪpjɚri/
a place where bees are kept
Example: The beekeeper manages several beehives in the apiary.

apiculture /ˈæpɪkˌʌltʃɚ/
the breeding and caring of bees
Example: The art of apiculture has been practiced for centuries.

apocalypse /əˈpɑkəˌlɪps/
an event of great destructive violence
Example: In the movie, a nuclear war triggered an apocalypse.

apology /əˈpɔləˌdʒi/
an expression of regret for some wrongdoing
Example: You need to offer a sincere apology.

apostrophe /əˈpɔstrəˌfi/
the punctuation mark (') used to indicate the omission of a letter or letters
Example: Our English teacher taught us how to use an apostrophe to show contraction.

the punctuation mark (') used to form the possessive
Example: In the sentence, "That is Sarah's book," the apostrophe indicates that the book belongs to Sarah.

apparatus /ˌɑpərɑtəs/
a collection of equipment used for a particular purpose
Example: The students poured the water in the apparatus.

appearance /ɑpˈɪrəns/
a sudden or unexpected arrival of someone or something at a place
Example: Her unexpected appearance at the party surprised everyone.

the introduction or invention of something

Example: The appearance of new technology revolutionised the way we communicate.

appendage /əˈpɛndɪdʒ/

a secondary part attached to a main part

Example: The spider uses its leg as an appendage to capture prey and move around.

appendix /ɑpˈɛndɪks/

separate additional material at the end of a book

Example: The author included an appendix with additional data and charts.

a short thin tube, closed at one end and attached to the large intestine at the other end

Example: Appendicitis is the inflammation of the appendix and may require surgical removal.

appetite /ˈɑpəˌtaɪt/

a desire for food or drink

Example: After a long day of hiking, their appetite was voracious.

appetizer /ˈɑpəˌtaɪzər/

a small amount of food or drink taken at the start of a meal to stimulate the appetite

Example: I ordered a vegetable salad as an appetizer before my main course.

applause /əˈplɔz/

appreciation shown by clapping one's hand

Example: The audience erupted into thunderous applause at the end of the captivating performance.

apple /ˈapəl/

a round firm fruit with red, yellow, or green skin and crisp whitish flesh, that grows on trees

Example: She took a bite of the crisp apple.

appliance /əˈplaɪəns/

a machine or device that has a specific function

Example: The firemen believed that the new appliance may have started the fire.

application /ˌaplɪkˈeɪʃən/

a formal request

Example: She submitted her application for the vacant position.

the act of applying something to a particular use

Example: The application of technology has revolutionised various industries.

appointment /apˈɔɪntmɛnt/

an arrangement to meet a person

Example: She scheduled an appointment with her dentist.

the act of placing someone in a position

Example: His promotion to the position of manager was a well-deserved appointment based on his skills and experience.

apprentice /əˈprɛntɪs/

someone who works for a skilled person for a fixed period to learn his or her own trade

Example: The young chef started as an apprentice in a renowned restaurant to gain experience.

approval /əˈpruvəl/

a favourable opinion

Example: The committee expressed their approval of the proposed project.

aquarium /əˈkwɛriəm/

a tank in which fish and other underwater creatures are kept

Example: The aquarium housed a diverse collection of colourful tropical fish.

aqueduct /ˈækwəˌdʌkt/

a structure, often a bridge, that carries water across a valley or river

Example: The city relies on the aqueduct to supply fresh water to its residents.

arabesque /ˌærəbˈɛsk/

a ballet position in which one leg is raised behind and the arms are extended

Example: The ballerina executed a beautiful arabesque.

arboretum /ˌɑrbɚˈitəm/

a botanical garden where rare trees or shrubs are cultivated

Example: The arboretum was a peaceful retreat, offering visitors a chance to explore diverse species of trees and enjoy nature.

arc /ˈɑrk/

a section of a circle or other curve

Example: The rainbow formed a vibrant arc in the sky after the rain shower.

area /ˈɛriə/

a section, part, or region

Example: The dining area of the restaurant was elegantly decorated.

a part having a specified function

Example: The storage area of the warehouse was organised and labelled for efficient inventory management.

the size of a two-dimensional surface

Example: The total area of the park was 15,000 square meters, providing ample space for recreational activities.

argument /ˈɑːrgjuːmənt/

a quarrel

Example: The students had an argument about a group project.

points presented to support or oppose a proposition

Example: The lawyer presented a compelling argument in favour of her client.

armchair /ˈɑːrmtʃɑːrmi/

the military land forces of a nation

Example: The army conducted military exercises to enhance their combat readiness.

many people or animals

Example: The army was deployed to the conflict zone to maintain peace and provide security.

arrival /ərˈaɪvəl/

the act of arriving

Example: The passengers eagerly awaited the arrival of their flight at the airport.

a person or thing that has just arrived

Example: The arrival of the package brought excitement as it contained the long-awaited gifts.

art /ˈɑːrt/

the creation of works of beauty with special significance

Example: She dedicated her life to the pursuit of art, creating spectacular paintings and sculptures.

any branch of the visual arts especially paintings

Example: The museum showcased a wide range of art.

article /ˈɑːrtɪkəl/

a written composition in a journal, magazine, or newspaper

Example: He wrote an informative article about the benefits of regular exercise.

aspect /ˈæspɛkt/

a distinct feature or element in a problem or situation

Example: The financial aspect of the project required meticulous budgeting.

a position facing a particular direction

Example: The balcony offered a stunning view of the city from an elevated aspect.

assignment /əsˈaɪnmənt/

something that has been assigned especially a task

Example: The teacher gave the students an assignment to complete over the weekend.

assistance /ɑsˈɪstəns/

help or support

Example: She offered her assistance to the elderly men.

assistant /ɑsˈɪstənt/

a helper or subordinate

Example: The CEO hired a competent assistant to manage his schedule.

association /ɑsˌoʊsɪˈeɪʃən/

a group of people with a common interest

Example: The photography association organised regular workshops.

a mental connection of ideas or feelings

Example: The smell of freshly baked cookies evoked pleasant childhood memories through association.

assumption /ɑsˈʌmpʃən/

something that is taken for granted

Example: Her assumption that he would be late proved to be incorrect as he arrived on time.

the act of assuming power or possession

Example: The company's assumption of a competitor's assets strengthened its market position.

atmosphere /ˈætməsfɪr/

the mass of gases surrounding the earth

Example: The Earth's atmosphere protects us from harmful radiation and provides the air we breathe.

the air in a particular place

Example: The cosy café had a welcoming atmosphere, with soft music and dim lighting.

a pervasive mood

Example: The tense atmosphere in the courtroom reflected the seriousness of the trial.

attempt /ɑˈtɛmpt/

an endeavour to achieve something

Example: She made an attempt to climb the steep mountain.

attention /ɑˈtɛnʃən/

concentrated direction of the mind

Example: He paid close attention to the teacher's instructions.

detailed care or treatment

Example: The patient received special attention from the medical team.

the alert position in a military drill

Example: The soldiers stood at attention, ready to receive commands from their officer.

attitude /ˈæɾɪtˌuːd/

the way a person thinks and behaves

Example: She had a positive attitude towards challenges.

attorney /əˈtɝni/

a person legally appointed to act for another

Example: The attorney represented the defendant in court.

attraction /əˈtɹækʃən/

the act or quality of attracting

Example: The amusement park had many thrilling rides that were the main attraction for visitors.

attrition /əˈtɹɪʃən/

constant wearing down to weaken or destroy

Example: The attrition of the company's customer base was a cause for concern.

auction /ˈɔkʃən/

a public sale at which articles are sold to the highest bidder

Example: The rare painting was sold at a high price during the art auction.

auctioneer /ˌɔkʃəˈnɪɹ/

a person who conducts auctions

Example: The skilled auctioneer efficiently managed the bidding.

audience /ˈɔːdiəns/

a group of spectators at a concert or play

Example: The audience clapped and cheered after the musicians' outstanding performance.

audiometer /ˌɔːdiˈoʊmɪɚ/

an instrument for testing hearing

Example: The audiologist used the audiometer to assess the patient's hearing thresholds.

audit /ˈɔdɪt/

an official inspection of business accounts, conducted by an independent qualified accountant

Example: The company hired an auditing firm to perform an annual audit and ensure financial accuracy.

auditor /ˈɔdɪtɚ/

a person qualified to audit accounts

Example: The auditor carefully reviewed the company's financial statements.

auditorium /ˌɔdəˈtɔriəm/

the area of a concert hall or theatre in which the audience sits

Example: The newly renovated auditorium could accommodate thousands of people.

auger /ˈɔgɚ/

a pointed tool for boring holes

Example: I used an auger to bore holes for planting fence posts.

aunt /ˈænt/

a sister of one's father or mother

Example: My aunt, Lisa, is visiting us this weekend.

the wife of one's uncle

Example: My uncle recently got married, so his wife is now my aunt.

aura /ˈɔɹə/

a distinctive air or quality associated with a person or thing

Example: The artist's paintings exude a mysterious aura that captivates viewers.

author /ˈɔθɚ/

a person who writes a book, article, or other written work

Example: J.K. Rowling is a renowned author known for her bestselling Harry Potter series.

authority /əˈθɔrəti/

the power to command

Example: The police officer has the authority to enforce the law and maintain order in the city.

autism /ˈɔˌtɪzəm/

abnormal self-absorption characterized by lack of response to people and limited ability to communicate

Example: Children with autism often have unique strengths and challenges.

autocracy /ɔˈtɑkrəsi/

government by an individual with unrestricted authority

Example: The country is ruled by an autocracy, with all power concentrated in the hands of a single leader.

autocrat /ˈɔtəˌkræt/

a ruler with absolute authority

Example: The autocrat ruled with an iron fist.

autograph /ˈɔtəˌgræf/

a handwritten signature of a famous person

Example: I was thrilled to receive an autograph from my favourite actor.

autopsy /ˈɔˌtɑpsi/

examination of a corpse to determine the cause of death

Example: The medical examiner conducted an autopsy to determine the cause of death.

autumn /ˈɔtəm/

the season of the year between summer and winter

Example: The leaves turn vibrant shades of orange and red in autumn.

avarice /ˈævɚəs/

extreme greed for wealth

Example: His avarice drove him to accumulate vast amounts of wealth.

average /ˈævrɪdʒ/

the typical or normal amount or quality

Example: The weather this week has been quite pleasant, with temperatures hovering around the average for this time of year.

the result obtained by adding the numbers in a set and dividing the total by the number of members in the set

Example: The test average is 80.

aversion /əˈvɝʒən/

extreme dislike or disinclination

Example: I have an aversion to spiders and feel uneasy whenever I see one.

aviation /ˌeɪviˈeɪʃən/

the art or science of flying aircraft

Example: My dream is to become a pilot and pursue a career in aviation.

awareness /ɑwˈɛrnəs/

being informed about a topic or subject

Example: The campaign aims to raise awareness about the effects of global warming.

awe /ˈɔː/

wonder and respect mixed with dread

Example: Standing on the edge of the Grand Canyon, I could not help but feel a sense of awe and wonder.

axe /ˈæks/

a hand tool with one side of its head sharpened to a cutting edge.

Example: The lumberjack swung the axe with precision.

axil /ˈæksɪl/

the angle where the stalk of a leaf joins a stem

Example: The axil of the plant is where the leaf attaches to the stem.

axiom /ˈæksiəm/

a generally accepted principle

Example: The axiom "less is more" suggests that simplicity and minimalism often yield better results.

axle /ˈæksəl/

a shaft on which a wheel or pair of wheels revolves

Example: The car's axle snapped, causing the wheel to come loose.

azure /ˈæʒɚ/

the deep blue colour of a clear blue sky

Example: The sky was a brilliant shade of azure, creating a stunning backdrop for the sunset.

Bb

baby /bˈeɪbi/
a newborn child or animal
Example: The baby slept soundly in the crib.
the youngest of a family or group
Example: She is the baby of the family.

back /bˈæk/
the rear part of the human body, from the neck to the pelvis
Example: He had a tattoo on his back.
the part or position of an object opposite the front
Example: The cover at the back is well-designed.

background /bˈækgraʊnd/
the events or circumstances that help to explain something
Example: Her troubled childhood provided a difficult background for her success.
a person's social class, education, or experience
Example: He comes from a wealthy background with a prestigious education.

bacon /bˈeɪkən/
meat from the back and sides of a pig, dried, salted, and often smoked
Example: I love the smell of sizzling bacon in the morning.

bag /bˈɑg/
flexible container with an opening to the end
Example: He packed his belongings in a duffel bag.
a piece of luggage
Example: She checked in her bag before boarding the flight.
a loose fold of skin under the eyes

Example: She used an eye cream to reduce the appearance of the bag under her right eye.

bakery /bˈeɪkə-ri/

place where bread, cakes, etc. are made or sold

Example: I bought a loaf of fresh bread from the local bakery.

balance /bˈæləns/

stability of mind or body

Example: Yoga helps improve balance and flexibility.

a state of being stable

Example: Finding a work-life balance is important for overall well-being.

ball /bˈɔːl/

a spherical or nearly spherical mass

Example: We played a game of soccer with a ball in the park.

balloon /bəlˈuːn/

an inflatable rubber bag used as a party decoration

Example: The boy enjoyed playing with colourful balloon.

a large bag inflated with a lighter-than-air gas, designed to rise and float in the atmosphere with a basket to carry passengers

Example: She had never been in a hot air balloon before.

bank /bˈaŋk/

an institution offering services of safekeeping and lending money at an interest

Example: He opened a savings account at the local bank.

a long-raised mass, especially of earth

Example: They sat on the bank of the river and enjoyed the view of the water.

the sloping side and ground on either side of the river

Example: The hikers climbed to the top of the steep bank to get a better vantage point.

baron /bˈærən/

a member of the lowest rank of nobility in the British Isles

Example: The baron and his family resided in a grand estate.

a powerful businessman or financier

Example: The oil baron made a fortune through his investments in the energy sector.

barracks /bˈɛrəks/

a building or group of buildings used to accommodate military personnel

Example: The soldiers were housed in the barracks during their training.

baseball /bˈeɪsbɔːl/

a team game in which the objective is to score runs by batting the ball and run round all four bases

Example: My favourite sport is baseball.

basis /bˈeɪsɪs/

something that underlies, or supports an idea, or belief

Example: The company's decision was made on the basis of market research.

basket /bˈæskɪt/

a container made of interwoven strips of wood or cane

Example: She filled the basket with fresh fruits and vegetables.

bath /bˈæθ/

a large container in which to wash the body

Example: I like to relax in a warm bath after a long day.

bathroom /bˈæθruːm/

a room with a bath or shower, washbasin, and toilet

Example:	The hotel room had a spacious bathroom with a bathtub and a shower.

battlefield /bˈærəlfˌiːld/

the place where a battle is fought

Example:	The soldiers fought bravely on the battlefield.

bean /bˈiːn/

the seed or pod of various climbing plants, eaten as a vegetable

Example:	He choked on a soya bean and died suddenly.

bear /bˈɛr/

a large heavily built mammal with a long shaggy coat

Example:	We saw a bear while hiking in the forest.

an ill-mannered person

Example:	He acted like a bear, growling at everyone, and refusing to cooperate.

a person who sells shares in anticipation of fallen prices to make a profit on repurchases

Example:	The bear predicted a market downturn and sold all his stocks.

beauty /bjˈuːti/

the combination of all the qualities of a person or thing that delight the senses and mind

Example:	The sunset over the ocean was a breathtaking display of beauty.

bed /bˈɛd/

a piece of furniture on which to sleep

Example:	I was so tired after work that I fell asleep as soon as my head hit the bed.

a plot of land in which plants are grown

Example:	The farmer tended to his main vegetable bed.

the bottom of a river, lake, or sea

Example: Divers explored the coral reefs on the ocean bed.

bedroom /bˈɛdruːm/

a room used for sleeping

Example: I share a bedroom with my brother.

beer /bˈɪr/

an alcoholic drink brewed from malt, sugar, hops, and water.

Example: This beer has been brewed using traditional methods.

beginning /bɪgˈɪnɪŋ/

the place where or time when something starts

Example: The beginning of the movie had an intense and suspenseful opening scene.

belief /bɪlˈiːf/

trust or confidence

Example: His unwavering belief in himself and his abilities helped him overcome many challenges.

benefactor /bˈɛnɪfˌæktɚ/

a person who supports a person or institution by giving money

Example: The generous benefactor donated a substantial amount to the charity.

benefit /bˈɛnɪfˌɪt/

something that improves or promotes

Example: Taking breaks during work hours can be a benefit to productivity.

a payment made by an institution or government to a person who is ill, unemployed, etc.

Example: He received no unemployment benefit while searching for a new job

bird /bˈɜːd/

a two-legged creature with feathers and wings, which lays eggs and can usually fly

Example: *Parrot is a beautiful tropical bird.*

birth /bˈɜːθ/

the process of bearing young

Example: *The midwife assisted with the birth of the baby.*

birthday /bˈɜːθdeɪ/

an anniversary of the day of one's birth

Example: *We celebrated her 30th birthday with a surprise party.*

bit /bˈɪt)/

a small piece, portion, or quantity

Example: *He gave me a bit of advice.*

a short time or distance

Example: *Wait here for a bit, I will be right back.*

a metal mouthpiece on a bridle for controlling a horse

Example: *He gently tugged on the horse's bit to signal a turn.*

a cutting or drilling tool

Example: *The carpenter used a drill bit to create holes.*

blender /blˈɛndɚ/

an electric kitchen appliance for pureeing
vegetables etc.

Example: *She used a blender to make a smoothie.*

blood /blˈʌd/

a reddish fluid in vertebrates that is pumped by the heart through the arteries and veins

Example: *The nurse took a sample of blood for testing.*

blouse /blˈaʊz/

a woman's shirt-like garment

Example: She wore a silk blouse to work.

board /bˈoːrd/

a long, wide, flat piece of sawn timber

Example: The carpenter used a board to construct the shelves.

a group of people who officially administer a company, trust, etc.

Example: The board of directors oversees the strategic decisions of the company.

boat /bˈoʊt/

a small vessel propelled by oars, paddle, sails, or motor

Example: We went fishing in a small boat.

body /bˈɔːdi/

the entire physical structure of an animal or human

Example: The human body consists of various organs and systems.

a group regarded as a single entity

Example: The committee acted as a single body in making decisions.

bonus /bˈoʊnəs/

something given, paid, or received above what is due or expected

Example: The employees received a bonus for their exceptional performance.

book /bˈʊk/

several printed pages bound together along one edge and protected by covers

Example: I read my favourite book numerous times.

boss /bˈɔs/

a person in charge of or employing others

Example: The boss praised the team for completing the project ahead of schedule.

a raised knob or stud, especially an ornamental one on a vault, shield, etc.

Example: The metal door had a large, ornate boss at its centre.

botany /bˈɔːtəni/

the study of plants

Example: She pursued a degree in botany to learn more about plant species and their characteristics.

bottom /bˈɔtəm/

the lowest, deepest, or farthest removed part of a thing

Example: The treasure was buried at the bottom of the sea.

the underneath part of something

Example: I found my missing earring at the bottom of my handbag.

bow /bˈoʊ/

a decorative knot usually having two loops and two loose ends

Example: She tied a beautiful bow on top of the gift box.

a weapon for shooting arrows

Example: With practice and strength, she learned to wield the bow effectively.

the front part of a vessel

Example: The ship's bow sliced through the waves as it sailed towards the horizon.

box /bˈɔːks/

a container with a firm base and sides and sometimes a removable or hinged lid

Example: She packed her belongings in a cardboard box for moving.

a slow-growing evergreen tree or shrub with small shiny leaves

Example: The neatly trimmed box provided a beautiful and elegant border for the garden.

boy /bˈɔɪ/

a male child

Example: The boy was running around the house.

a man regarded as immature or inexperienced

Example: Sometimes, my husband acts like a boy.

boyfriend /bˈɔɪfrɛnd/

a male friend with whom a person is usually romantically, or sexually involved

Example: My boyfriend is the most amazing person I know.

bread /brˈɛd/

a food made from a dough of flour mixed with water or milk, usually raised with yeast and then baked

Example: She made delicious homemade bread from scratch.

breath /brˈɛθ/

the taking in and letting out of air during breathing

Example: After running, she took a deep breath.

short pause or rest

Example: He took a breath before delivering his speech.

bridge /brˈɪdʒ/

a structure that provides a way over a railway, river, etc.

Example: The suspension bridge spanned across the river.

a dental plate containing artificial teeth that is secured to natural teeth

Example: The dentist fitted him with a bridge to replace his missing teeth.

briefcase /brˈiːfkeɪs/

a flat portable case for carrying books, papers, etc.

Example: The CEO's briefcase is stolen.

brother /brˈʌðɚ/

a man or boy with the same parents as another person

Example: My brother is very muscular.

bucket /bˈʌkɪt/

an open-topped cylindrical container with a handle

Example: She filled the bucket with water.

building /bˈɪldɪŋ/

a structure with a roof and walls

Example: Burj Khalifa is the tallest building in the world.

bull /bˈʊl/

a male of various animals including domestic cattle, elephant, and whale

Example: The rancher owned a black bull for breeding purposes.

a very large, strong, or aggressive person

Example: He is a bull of a man, capable of lifting heavy weights effortlessly.

a ludicrously, self-contradictory, or nonsensical statement

Example: His argument was full of bull; none of it made any logical sense.

a formal document issued by the pope

Example: The papal bull outlined new policies for the Catholic Church.

bunch /bˈʌnt͡ʃ/

several things growing, fastened, or grouped together

Example: My mother purchased a bunch of bananas from the market.

bus /bˈʌs/

a large motor vehicle designed to carry passengers between stopping places along a regular route

Example: She takes the bus to school every morning.

business /bˈɪznəs/

the purchase and sale of goods and services

Example: She owns a small business in the city.

butterfly /bˈʌɾɚ-flˌaɪ/

an insect with a slender body and brightly coloured wings

Example: The butterfly landed delicately on the flower.

buyer /bˈaɪɚ/

a person who buys, a customer

Example: The buyer examined the cellular phone before purchasing.

Cc

cabinet /kˈæbɪnət/

a piece of furniture containing shelves, cupboards, or drawers for storage or display

Example: My mother hides her money in the cabinet.

calf /kˈæf/

a young cow, bull, elephant, whale, or seal

Example: The calf is sick.

the back of the leg between the ankle and the knee

Example: After strenuous exercising, my left calf hurts terribly.

calm /kˈɑːm/

a peaceful state

Example: After a long and stressful day, she found solace in the calm of the ocean.

camera /kˈæmrə/

a piece of equipment used for taking photographs or pictures for television or cinema

Example: My camera fell in the water.

campus /kˈampəs/

the grounds and buildings of a university or college

Example: They repainted the campus.

cancer /kˈænsɚ/

a serious disease resulting from a malignant growth or tumour, caused by abnormal and uncontrolled cell division

Example: Many scientists are searching for a cure of cancer.

candidate /kˈandɪdˌeɪt/

a person seeking a job or position

Example: The employers expressed that Alice is a suitable candidate for the job.

a person taking an examination

Example: Mary is a candidate for the medical school admission exam.

candy /kˈandi/

a sweet or sweets

Example: This candy is coated with ginger.

cap /kˈap/

a soft close-fitting covering for the head

Example: I purchased a fancy cap for the games.

a small flat lid

Example: Ensure you place the cap on the bottle after using it.

a contraceptive device placed over the mouth of the womb

Example: Her cervical cap was poorly placed, so she became pregnant.

capital /kˈapɪrəl/

the chief city of a country

Example: Georgetown is the capital of Guyana.

the total wealth owned or used in a business by an individual or group

Example: The shareholders are asked to invest more capital in the business.

car /kˈɑːɹ/

a motorized road vehicle designed to carry a small number of people

Example: I travel to school by car.

card /kˈɑːɹd/

a piece of stiff paper or thin cardboard used for identification, reference, proof of membership, or sending greetings or messages

Example: Your birthday card means a lot.

one of a set of small pieces of cardboard, marked with figures or symbols, used for playing games or for fortune-telling

Example: She pulled a tarot card from the deck and read the message on it.

care /kˈɛr/

careful or serious attention; cautions

Example: Accountants are required to exert due care when preparing financial statements.

career /kɚrˈɪr/

the series of jobs in a profession or occupation that a person has through his or her life

Example: She is now focusing on her career as a photographer.

case /kˈeɪs/

a single instance or example of something

Example: The teacher gave us a case to study in preparation for the upcoming exam.

a matter for a discussion

Example: The new policy was a case for debate among the members of the committee.

a set of arguments supporting an action or cause

Example: The lawyer presented a compelling case in support of her client.

a person dealt with by a doctor, social worker, or solicitor

Example: The social worker was assigned a case involving a family in need of assistance.

an action or lawsuit

Example: The plaintiff's case was dismissed due to lack of evidence.

cash /kˈɑʃ/

banknotes and coins rather than cheques

Example: The cashier placed the cash in a drawer.

cat /kˈɑt/

a small, domesticated mammal with thick, soft fur and whiskers

Example: I have a beautiful, brown cat.

category /kˈɑtɪɡɚɹi/

a class or group of things or people with some quality or qualities in common

Example: I arranged my books on the bookshelf by category.

cause /kˈɔːz/

something that produces a particular effect

Example: The cause of the car accident was determined to be the driver's failure to stop at a red light.

grounds for action

Example: The poor working conditions were the cause of the workers' strike

caveman /kˈeɪvmən/

a prehistoric cave dweller

Example: The caveman emerged from the darkness of the cave.

celebration /sˌɛləbrˈeɪʃən/

the action of celebrating an important day or event

Example: We had a big celebration to mark my parents' 50th wedding anniversary.

cell /sˈɛl/

the smallest unit of an organism that can function independently

Example: The scientist observed the microscopic cell under the microscope.

a small simple room in a prison, convent, or monastery

Example: The prisoner was confined to a small cell with only a bed and a toilet.

a small group operating as the core of a larger organization

Example: The research team formed a core cell to develop the project.

a device that produces electrical energy by chemical action

Example: The portable charger uses a fuel cell to generate electricity.

census /sˈɛnsəs/

official periodic count of a population including such information as sex, age, and occupation

Example: The government conducts a census every ten years to gather demographic data.

chair /t͡ʃˈɛr/

a seat with a back and four legs, for one person to sit on

Example: I sat on the comfortable chair in the living room and began reading my book.

an official position of authority

Example: She was appointed as the chair of the committee.

championship /t͡ʃˈæmpiənʃˌɪp/

a contest for the position of champion in a sport or game

Example: The team trained hard and won the basketball championship.

chance /t͡ʃˈæns/

the extent to which something is likely to happen

Example: There is a good chance of rain tomorrow.

an opportunity or occasion to do something

Example: I am grateful for the chance to present my ideas at the conference.

a risk or gamble

Example: He took a chance and invested all his savings in the stock market.

chaos /kˈeɪɑːs/

complete disorder or confusion

Example: After the earthquake, there was chaos in the streets.

chapter /tʃˈaptɚ/

a division of a book

Example: I just finished reading the last chapter of the novel.

a period in a life or history

Example: The recent chapter of her life has been filled with success and happiness.

charity /tʃˈarɪti/

an organisation set up to provide help to those in need

Example: I donate to a local charity that supports homeless individuals.

cheek /tʃˈiːk/

either side of the face below the eye

Example: She gave him a kiss on the cheek as a sign of affection.

chef /ʃˈɛf/

a cook, usually a head cook, in a restaurant or hotel

Example: The chef was very friendly to his dinner guests.

chemistry /kˈɛmɪstri/

the branch of science concerned with the composition, properties, and reactions of substances

Example: She decided to pursue a degree in chemistry.

cherry /tʃˈɛri/

a small soft round fruit with red or blackish skin

Example: He picked a ripe cherry from the tree and enjoyed its sweet taste.

chest /tʃˈɛst/

the front of the body, from the neck to the waist

Example: He felt a tightness in his chest after running for a long time.

chicken /tʃˈɪkɪn/

a domestic fowl bred for its flesh and or eggs

Example: She cooked a delicious roasted chicken for dinner.

chief /tʃˈiːf/

the head of a group or body of people

Example: The chief of police addressed the concerns of the community during the meeting.

child /tʃˈaɪld/

a young human being; boy or girl

Example: The child is very aggressive.

childhood /tʃˈaɪldhʊd/

the time or condition of being a child

Example: She has fond memories of her childhood spent in the countryside.

children /tʃˈɪldrən/

a group of young human being

Example: The children giggled and played together in the playground.

chocolate /tʃˈɔːklət/

a food made from roasted ground cocoa seeds, usually sweetened, and flavoured

Example: I love dark chocolate.

choice /tʃˈɔɪs/

the act of choosing or selecting

Example: He had to make a difficult choice between two job offers.

a person or thing chosen or that may be chosen

Example: The red dress is my top choice for the party tonight.

choir /kwˈaɪɚ/

an organised group of singers, usually for singing in church

Example: The church choir performed a beautiful rendition of the hymn.

chopstick /t͡ʃˈɑːpstɪk/

a thin stick of ivory wood, or plastic, used for eating Chinese or other East Asian food

Example: She skilfully used one chopstick to pick up the apple.

church /t͡ʃɜːt͡ʃ/

a building for public Christian worship

Example: I go to the church every weekend.

cigarette /sˌɪɡɚˈɛt/

a thin roll of shredded tobacco in thin paper, for smoking

Example: He took a drag from his cigarette and exhaled a puff of smoke.

city /sˈɪti/

any large town

Example: This is a beautiful city.

clarity /klˈɑrɪti/

clearness

Example: The instructions provided clarity on how to assemble the furniture.

class /klˈɑs/

a group of people sharing a similar social and economic position

Example: The upper class in society often enjoys privileges and access to resources that others do not.

the system of dividing a society into such groups

Example: The caste system in some societies rigidly determines a person's class.

classmate /klˈɑsmeɪt/

a friend or contemporary in the same class of a school

Example: *My classmate is sick.*

classroom /klˈɑsruːm/

a room in a school where lessons take place

Example: *My classroom has many colourful teaching aids.*

cleverness /klˈɛvɚnəs/

the quality of being clever, intelligence, or showing good powers of judgement

Example: *His cleverness in solving puzzles impressed everyone.*

client /klˈaɪənt/

someone who uses the services of a professional person or organization

Example: *The lawyer's client was grateful for his dedicated representation.*

climate /klˈaɪmət/

the typical weather conditions of an area

Example: *The tropical climate of that region is known for its high temperatures and humidity.*

clothes /klˈoʊðz/

articles of dress

Example: *She bought new clothes for the upcoming party.*

clothing /klˈoʊðɪŋ/

garments collectively

Example: *She sorted through the pile of clothing, looking for something to wear to the party.*

coast /kˈoʊst/

the place where the land meets the sea

Example: They enjoyed a relaxing walk along the coast during their beach vacation.

cock /kˈɔːk/

a male bird, especially of domestic fowl

Example: The rooster is a type of cock that crows at sunrise.

the hammer of a gun

Example: He examined the intricate design on the handle of the cock before loading the gun.

coffee /kˈɔfi/

a drink made from the roasted and ground seeds of a tall tropical shrub

Example: Many students consume cups of coffee daily.

collection /kəlˈɛkʃən/

things collected or accumulated

Example: Her extensive collection of stamps includes rare and valuable specimens.

the act or process of collecting

Example: The collection of donations for the charity event took several weeks.

college /kˈɔlɪdʒ/

an institution of higher or further education that is not a university

Example: She enrolled in a liberal arts college to pursue her bachelor's degree.

combination /kˌɑːmbɪnˈeɪʃən/

the act of combining or the state of combining

Example: The recipe called for a combination of spices to enhance the flavour.

comeback /kˈʌmbæk/

a return to a former position or status

Example: After a year of absence, the athlete made a remarkable comeback in the competition.

committee /kəmˈɪti/

a group of people appointed to perform a specified service or function

Example: The committee was responsible for organizing the annual charity event.

communication /kəmjˌuːnɪkˈeɪʃən/

the exchange of information, ideas, or feelings

Example: Effective communication is key to maintaining healthy relationships.

community /kəmjˈuːnɪti/

all the people living in one district

Example: The local community came together to support the fundraising event.

a group of people with shared origins or interests

Example: The online gaming community is passionate about competitive multiplayer games.

company /kˈʌmpəni/

a business organisation

Example: I work for a software company.

the fact of being with someone

Example: Her dog provides her with constant company.

comparison /kəmpˈærɪsən/

comparing or being compared

Example: The comparison between the two cars revealed their differences in performance.

compassion /kəmpˈæʃən/

a feeling of distress and pity for the suffering or misfortune of another

Example: He showed great compassion towards the homeless and volunteered at a shelter.

competition /kˌɔːmpətˈɪʃən/

the act of competing

Example: The athletes trained hard in preparation for the upcoming competition.

complaint /kəmplˈeɪnt/

the act of complaining

Example: She filed a complaint with the customer service department about the faulty product.

computer /kəmpjˈuːrɚ/

an electronic device that processes data according to a set of instructions

Example: I use my computer for work and entertainment.

concept /kˈɔːnsɛpt/

an abstract or general idea

Example: The concept of justice is complex and subjective.

conclusion /kəŋklˈuːʒən/

a final decision, opinion, or judgement based on reasoning

Example: After careful analysis, they reached the conclusion that the project was not feasible.

end or ending

Example: The conclusion of the movie left the audience in suspense.

outcome or result

Example: The experiment's conclusion confirmed their hypothesis.

condition /kəndˈɪʃən/

a particular state of being

Example: The car was in excellent condition after being restored.

confidence /kˈɔːnfɪdəns/

trust in a person or thing

Example: She had confidence in her team's ability to succeed.

belief in one's own abilities

Example: His confidence allowed him to take on new challenges.

confusion /kənfjˈuːʒən/

mistaking one person or thing for another

Example: The identical twins often caused confusion among their friends.

connection /kənˈɛkʃən/

a relationship in which a person or thing is linked or associated with something else

Example: The Internet provides us with instant connection to people around the world.

consequence /kˈɔːnsɪkwəns/

a logical result or effect

Example: The consequence of her actions was losing her job.

significance or importance

Example: The consequence of his decision to drop out of college was a significant setback to his career prospects.

construction /kənstrˈʌkʃən/

the act of constructing or way a thing is constructed

Example: The construction of the new building will be completed by next year.

contact /kˈʌːntækt/

the state or act of communication

Example: I tried to establish contact with him, but he was unreachable.

the state or act of touching

Example: The child made contact with the hot stove and burned his hand.

an acquaintance who might be useful in business

Example: She reached out to her contacts in the industry to explore job opportunities.

contentment /kənt'ɛntmənt/

a state of happiness and satisfaction

Example: After a long day's work, she found contentment in curling up with a good book.

context /k'ɔːntɛkst/

the circumstances relevant to an event or fact

Example: It is important to consider the context of the conversation before jumping to conclusions.

contract /k'ʌːntrækt/

a formal agreement between two or more parties

Example: They signed a contract to outline the terms and conditions of their business partnership.

contribution /kˌɑːntrɪbj'uːʃən/

a gift or payment to a common fund or collection

Example: She made a generous contribution to the charity to support their cause.

a piece of writing submitted for publication in a journal, book, etc.

Example: Her contribution to the scientific journal was well-received and cited by other researchers.

the part played by a person or thing in bringing about a result or helping something to advance

Example: Each team member made a valuable contribution to the project's success.

control /kəntr'oʊl/

power to direct something

Example:	The manager has control over the decision-making process.

conversation /kɔːnvɚsˈeɪʃən/

talk between two or more people

Example:	This conversation is getting gloomy.

cooker /kˈʊkɚ/

an apparatus for cooking heated by gas or electricity

Example:	She prepared a delicious meal using the electric cooker.

cookie /kˈʊki/

a biscuit

Example:	I will share my cookie with you.

corpus /kˈɔːrpəs/

a collection of writings, such as one by a single author or on a specific topic

Example:	The researcher analysed a corpus of Shakespearean plays to study recurring themes.

cotton /kˈɔːtn̩/

the soft white downy fibre surrounding the seeds of a plant grown in warm climates, used to make cloth and thread

Example:	The textile industry heavily relies on cotton as a raw material for fabric production.

count /kˈaʊnt/

the act of counting

Example:	The count of the inventory revealed that there were 100 items in stock.

countdown /kˈaʊntdaʊn/

the act of counting backwards to zero to time exactly an operation such as the launching of a rocket

Example:	The countdown to the New Year's Eve fireworks display has begun.

country (kˈʌntri)

an area distinguished by its people, culture, language, or government

Example: She travelled to a foreign country to experience different cultures and traditions.

county /kˈaʊnti/

a division of a country

Example: He lives in a small town in the rural county.

courage /kˈɜːrɪdʒ/

the ability to face danger or pain without fear

Example: Despite her fear, she summoned the courage to confront her fears and speak up for herself.

course /kˈoːrs/

a complete series of lessons or lectures

Example: She enrolled in a photography course to improve her skills.

a sequence of medical treatment prescribed for a period

Example: The doctor recommended a six-week course of antibiotics to treat the infection.

a route or direction taken

Example: The hikers followed the mountain trail as their course to reach the summit.

cousin /kˈʌzən/

the child of one's aunt or uncle

Example: My cousin does not like cats.

cow /kˈaʊ/

the mature female of various mammals, such as cattle, elephant, or whale

Example: I have a pet cow.

craft /krˈæft/

an occupation requiring skill or manual dexterity

Example: This is a beautiful craft.

credit /krˈɛdɪt/

the system of allowing customers to receive goods or services before payment

Example: He purchased the new laptop on credit.

crest /krˈɛst/

the top of a mountain, hill, or wave

Example: They reached the crest of the hill and enjoyed the scenic view.

a tuft of growth of feathers or skin on the top of a bird's or animal's head

Example: The peacock proudly displayed its colourful crest.

a heraldic design or figure used on a coat of arms and elsewhere

Example: The family crest features a lion and a crown.

crew /krˈuː/

the people who man a ship or aircraft

Example: The crew prepared the plane for take-off.

a group of people working together

Example: The film crew worked tirelessly to bring the director's vision to life.

crime /krˈaɪm/

an act prohibited and punished by law

Example: He is punished for the crime committed.

criticism /krˈɪtɪsˌɪzəm/

fault-finding or censure

Example: He received constructive criticism on his writing to help him improve.

an analysis of a work done, such as literature

Example: The literary criticism examined the themes and symbolism in the novel.

crowd /krˈaʊd/

many things or people gathered

Example: The concert drew a huge crowd of enthusiastic fans.

cuff /kˈʌf/

the end of a sleeve

Example: The cuff on this shirt is too tight.

culture /kˈʌltʃɚ/

the ideas, customs, and art of a particular society

Example: The festival showcased the rich culture and traditions of the indigenous community.

cupboard /kˈʌbəd/

a piece of furniture or a recess with a door, for storage

Example: She organised her kitchen supplies in the cupboard.

currency /kˈɜːrənsi/

the actual coins or banknotes in use in a particular country

Example: The local currency is the Euro in that country.

customer /kˈʌstəmɚ/

a person who buys goods or services

Example: The customer examined the products before purchasing them.

cycle /sˈaɪkəl/

a complete series of recurring events

Example: We learnt the business cycle in school yesterday.

Dd

dad /dˈɑd/
father
Example: *My dad taught me how to swim.*

dance /dˈɑns/
a social meeting arranged for dancing
Example: *They attended a dance at the community centre.*

danger /dˈeɪndʒɚ/
the possibility that someone may be injured or killed
Example: *Climbing steep cliffs without safety equipment is a danger.*
someone or something that may cause injury or harm
Example: *The wild animals in the forest can be a danger if approached without caution.*

daredevil /dˈɛrdɛvəl/
a recklessly bold person
Example: *The daredevil performed daring stunts on his motorcycle.*

data /dˈeɪtə/
a series of observations, measurements, or facts
Example: *The scientist collected data from the experiment to analyse and draw conclusions.*
the numbers, digits, characters, and symbols operated on by a computer
Example: *The computer program processed a large amount of data to generate the final report.*

database /dˈeɪtəˌeɪs/
a store of information in a form that can be easily handled by a computer
Example: *The company maintains a customer database to track orders and contact information.*

date /dˈeɪt/

a specified day of the month

Example:　　Today's date is May 11th.

an appointment, especially with a person to whom one is romantically attached

Example:　　He asked her out on a date to the movies.

day /dˈeɪ/

the period of 24 hours from one midnight to the next

Example:　　The school day starts at 8 am and ends at 3 pm.

the period of light between sunrise and sunset

Example:　　They spent the day at the beach.

daydream /dˈeɪdriːm/

a pleasant fantasy indulged in while awake

Example:　　During class, she often drifted off into a daydream.

dealer /dˈiːlɚ/

a person or organization whose business involves buying and selling things

Example:　　He works as a car dealer.

death /dˈɛθ/

the permanent end of life in a person or animal

Example:　　Her death shocked everyone.

debt /dˈɛt/

a sum of money owed

Example:　　He is struggling to repay his student loan debt.

decision /dɪsˈɪʒən/

a choice or judgement made about something.

Example:　　After careful consideration, she made the decision to accept the job offer.

deer /dˈɪr/
a large-hoofed mammal
Example: We spotted a herd of deer.

definition /dˌɛfɪnˈɪʃən/
a statement of the meaning of a word or phrase
Example: The teacher provided clear a definition for the given term.
a description of the essential qualities of something
Example: The definition of success may vary from person to person.
sharpness of outline
Example: The artist emphasised the definition of the subject by capturing its sharpness of outline.

delivery /dɪlˈɪvɚri/
the act of delivering goods or mail
Example: The package was scheduled for delivery today.
the act of giving birth to a baby.
Example: The doctor assisted with the safe delivery of the new-born.
manner or style in public speaking
Example: Her confident delivery captivated the audience.

demand /dɪmˈænd/
a forceful request
Example: The protesters made a demand for justice and accountability.
something that requires special effort or sacrifice
Example: The demand for perfection in her work was relentless.
the amount of commodity that consumers are willing and able to buy at a specified price.
Example: The demand for luxury cars has been increasing steadily.

dentist /dˈɛntɪst/
a person qualified to practice dentistry
Example: I have an appointment with the dentist tomorrow.

department /dɪpˈɑːrtmənt/

a specialized division of a large business organisation, hospital, university, etc.

Example: She works in the marketing department.

departure /dɪpˈɑːrtʃɚ/

the act of departing

Example: The departure of the train was delayed by 30 minutes.

a divergence from previous custom, rule, etc.

Example: His artistic style represents a departure from traditional norms.

depression /dɪprˈɛʃən/

a mental state in which a person has feeling of gloom and inadequacy

Example: She sought therapy to help her overcome her depression.

an economic condition in which there is substantial unemployment, low output, and investment

Example: The Great Depression of the 1930s had a significant impact on the global economy.

depth /dˈɛpθ/

the distance downwards, backwards, or inwards

Example: The swimming pool has a depth of 2 meters.

the quality of having a high degree of knowledge, insight, and understanding

Example: Her depth of understanding on the subject impressed the professor.

intensity of emotion or feeling

Example: The movie evoked a range of emotions with its depth of storytelling.

description /dɪskrˈɪpʃən/

a statement or account that describes someone or something

Example: The book provided a vivid description of the beautiful landscape.

design /dɪzˈaɪn/

a sketch, plan, or preliminary drawing

Example: The architect created a detailed design of the new building.

the arrangement of an artistic work

Example: The design of the painting was intricate and visually appealing.

designer /dɪzˈaɪnɚ/

a person who draws up original sketches or plans from which things are made

Example: She is a fashion designer known for her innovative and unique designs.

desk /dˈɛsk/

a piece of furniture with a writing surface and usually drawers

Example: I have a tidy desk where I do my work.

the section of a newspaper or television station responsible for a particular subject

Example: The sports desk of the newspaper covers all the latest sports news.

detective /dɪtˈɛktɪv/

a police officer who investigates crimes

Example: Jade is a new detective.

development /dɪvˈɛləpmənt/

the process of growing or developing

Example: The company focuses on the development of new technologies.

an event or incident that changes a situation

Example: The sudden increase in demand was a significant development for the business.

device /dɪvˈaɪs/

a machine or tool used for a particular purpose

Example: The smartphone is a popular electronic device used for communication.

a scheme or plan

Example: The marketing team came up with a new advertising device to promote the product.

diamond /dˈaɪəmənd/

a usually colourless exceptionally hard precious stone of crystalized carbon

Example: She wore a beautiful diamond necklace for her wedding.

difference /dˈɪfrəns/

the state or quality of being unlike

Example: The difference between the two paintings is striking.

a disagreement or argument

Example: They had a difference of opinion regarding the best approach to the project.

the result of the subtraction of one number or quantity from another

Example: The difference between 10 and 6 is 4.

difficulty /dˈɪfɪkˌʌlti/

the state or quality that is hard to deal with

Example: He faced great difficulty in solving the complex math problem.

an objection or obstacle

Example: The major difficulty we encountered during the project was a lack of funding.

dinner /dˈɪnɚ/

the main meal of the day, usually eaten in the evening

Example: Dad prepared dinner for the family.

a formal social occasion at which an evening meal is served

Example: The couple went out for a romantic dinner.

direction /daɪrˈɛkʃən/

the course or line along which a person or thing moves, points, or lies

Example: The sign pointed in the direction of the nearest town.

management or guidance

Example: The company needs strong direction to navigate through the challenges.

the work of a stage or film director

Example: The direction in this play was exceptional, bringing out the best in the actors.

director /daɪrˈɛktɚ/

a person or thing that directs or controls

Example: The director of the company made important decisions regarding its strategy.

a member of the government board of a business

Example: The director oversees the operations of the company.

the person responsible for the artistic and technical aspects of the making of a film

Example: The film director worked closely with the actors and crew to bring the script to life on screen.

dirt /dˈɜːt/

any unclean substance, such as mud

Example: The children played in the dirt and got their clothes dirty.

loose earth; soil

Example: The gardener dug into the dirt to plant new flowers.

obscene speech or writing

Example: The comedian's jokes were filled with dirt and made the audience laugh.

disaster /dɪzˈæstɚ/

an accident that causes great distress or destruction

Example: The earthquake was a disaster that left many people homeless.

something that fails or has been ruined

Example: The party turned into a disaster when it started raining heavily.

discipline /dˈɪsɪplˌɪn/

the practice of imposing strict rules of behaviour on other people

Example: The teacher maintains discipline in the classroom by setting clear expectations.

the ability to work in a behaved and controlled manner

Example: Martial arts training instils discipline in practitioners.

a particular area of academic study

Example: He pursued a degree in the field of social sciences and focused on the discipline of sociology.

discussion /dɪskˈʌʃən/

the action or process of talking about something to reach a decision or to exchange ideas

Example: The team gathered for a discussion to brainstorm ideas for the project.

a detailed treatment of a topic in speech or writing

Example: The professor gave a thorough discussion of the theories in his research paper.

disease /dɪzˈiːz/

an unhealthy condition in a person, animal, or plant which is caused by bacteria or infection

Example: The flu is a contagious disease.

dish /dˈɪʃ/

a container used for holding or serving food

Example: She placed the delicious curry in a serving dish.

a particular kind of food

Example: Sushi is a popular Japanese dish.

disk /dˈɪsk/

a storage device, consisting of a stack of plates coated with a magnetic layer, which rotates rapidly as a single unit

Example: The computer's hard disk stores all the data and files.

distribution /dˌɪstrɪbjˈuːʃən/

the delivery of leaflets, mail, etc. to individual people or organizations

Example: The distribution of leaflets was carried out by a team of volunteers.

dog /dˈɔːg/

a domesticated canine mammal occurring in many different breeds

Example: My dog loves to play fetch in the park.

domino /dˈɒmɪnˌoʊ/

a small rectangular block marked with dots, used in dominoes.

Example: He placed a domino on the table.

donkey /dˈɒŋki/

a long-eared member of the horse family

Example: The farmer used a donkey to carry heavy loads on his farm.

a person who is stupid or stubborn

Example: Stop being such a donkey and listen to reason.

dragonfly /drˈægənflˌaɪ/

a brightly coloured insect with a long slender body and a pair of wings

Example: The dragonfly hovered over the pond.

drake /drˈeɪk/

the male of a duck

Example: The drake swam gracefully in the pond.

drama /drˈɑːmə/

a serious play for theatre, television, etc

Example: The local theatre group put on an engaging drama that captivated the audience.

a situation that is exciting or highly emotional

Example: The family reunion turned into a drama when old conflicts resurfaced.

drawer /drˈɔːr/

a sliding box-shaped part of a piece of furniture used for storage

Example: She opened the top drawer of her desk to retrieve a pen.

a person or thing that draws

Example: The artist is a skilled drawer, capturing intricate details in their sketches.

drawing /drˈɔːɪŋ/

a picture or plan made by means of lines on a surface

Example: The child proudly showed their drawing of a sunny day.

dresser /drˈɛsɚ/

a piece of furniture with shelves and cupboards, used for storing or displaying dishes

Example: The antique dresser in the dining room showcased a collection of fine China.

a person who dresses in a specified way

Example: She is a fashion-forward dresser, always wearing the latest trends.

a person employed to assist performers with their costumes

Example: The theatre hired a professional dresser to ensure quick costume changes during the production.

driver /drˈaɪvɚ/

a person who drives a vehicles

Example: The taxi driver took us to the airport.

a long-shafted club with a large head and a steep face, used for tee shots

Example: He swung the driver and sent the golf ball soaring through the air.

drum /drˈʌm/

a percussion instrument sounded by striking a skin stretched across the opening of a hollow cylinder

Example: The drummer set the rhythm with his energetic beats on the drum.

duchess /dˈʌt͡ʃɛs/

a woman who holds the rank of a duke

Example: The duchess attended the royal banquet wearing an elegant gown.

the wife or widow of a duke

Example: The late duke's funeral was attended by the grieving duchess.

duck /dˈʌk/

a water bird with short legs, webbed feet, and a broad blunt bill

Example: The duck gracefully glided across the pond.

the female of such a bird

Example: The mother duck led her ducklings across the field.

duke /dˈuːk/

a nobleman of the highest rank

Example: The duke presided over the council, making important decisions for the kingdom.

duty /dˈuːti/

the work performed as part of one's job

Example: The police officer diligently carried out his duty to protect and serve the community.

an obligation to fulfil one's responsibility

Example: It is our duty as citizens to vote in the upcoming election.

a government tax on imports

Example: The customs imposed a heavy duty on imported goods.

Ee

ear /ˈɪɪ/

the part of the body with which a person or animal hears

Example: He put his hands over his ears.

willingness to listen

Example: You need a good ear to master the piano.

the part of a cereal plant, such as wheat or barley, that contains the seed

Example: We were lucky to see one ear of corn on a stalk.

earth /ˈɜːθ/

the planet that we live on, the third planet from the sun, the only planet on which life is known to exist

Example: The earth revolves around the sun.

echo /ˈɛkoʊ/

the reflection of sound by a solid object

Example: The hills sent back a faint echo.

a repetition of someone else's opinions

Example: His words were an echo of what she had heard many times before.

economics /ˌiːkənˈɑːmɪks/

the study of the production and consumption of goods and services and the commercial activities of a society

Example: The economics of the project are very doubtful.

economy /ɪkˈɑːnəmi/

the system by which the production, distribution, and consumption of goods and services organized in a country or community.

Example: The world economy is still suffering from the effects of the pandemic.

the ability of a country to generate wealth through business and industry.

Example: The country's economy grew at an annual rate of more than 10 per cent.

editor /ˈɛdɪrɚ/

a person in overall charge of a newspaper, magazine, or a television or radio programme.

Example: He is a former editor of the journal.

education /ˌɛdʒuːkˈeɪʃən/

the process of acquiring knowledge and understanding

Example: The school provides an excellent all-round education

effect /ɪfˈɛkt/

a change or situation caused by something or someone

Example: Her tears had no effect on him.

power to influence or produce a result

Example: His protest had no effect.

the condition of being operative

Example: The law goes into effect next week.

efficiency /ɪfˈɪʃənsi/

the quality or state of being efficient

Example: The factory was operating at peak efficiency.

effort /ˈɛfɚt/

physical or mental energy needed to do something

Example: You should put more effort into your work.

achievements or creations

Example: The book was her finest effort.

egg /ˈɛg/

the oval or round object laid by the females of birds, reptiles, and other creatures, containing a developing embryo

Example: The hen sits on the eggs until they hatch.

a type of cell produced in the body of a female animal which can develop into a baby if fertilized by a male reproductive cell

Example: The male sperm fertilizes the female egg.

election /ɨlˈɛkʃən/

a process whereby people vote for a person or party to fill a position

Example: Elections will be held later this year.

elevator /ˈɛlɪvˌeɪɾɚ/

a lift for carrying people

Example: The elevator is stuck on the fourth floor of the hotel.

elf /ˈɛlf/

a small mischievous fairy

Example: The elf surprised the shoemaker.

emotion /ɪmˈoʊʃən/

any strong feeling, such as joy or fear

Example: Fear is a normal human emotion.

the part of a person's character based on feelings rather than thought

Example: Her voice trembled with emotion.

emperor /ˈɛmpɚɹɚ/

a man who rules an empire

Example: It was up to the emperor to cast the deciding vote.

emphasis /ˈɛmfəsɪs/

special importance or significance given to something

Example: There is too much emphasis on reducing costs.

stress on a particular syllable, word, or phrase in speaking

Example: He placed extra emphasis on the word 'never'.

employee /ɛmplˈɔɪiː/

a person who is hired to work for someone in return of payment

Example: The company has over 500 employees.

employer /ɛmplˈɔɪɚ/

a person or company that hires workers

Example: The law requires employers to offer a safe work environment.

employment /ɛmplˈɔɪmənt/

the act of employing or state of being employed

Example: She was unable to find employment.

a person's work or occupation

Example: He regularly drove from his home to his place of employment.

the availability of jobs for the population of a town, country, etc.

Example: They are finding it more and more difficult to find employment.

empress /ˈɛmpɹɛs/

a woman who rules an empire

Example: Queen Victoria was Empress of India as well as Queen of Great Britain.

the wife or widow of an emperor

Example: Empress Josephine's marriage to Napoleon was dissolved in 1809.

enchanter /ɛntʃˈæntɚ/

a person who uses magic, especially to put someone or something under a spell

Example: He is like a serpent enchanter.

end /ˈɛnd/

one of the two extreme points of something such as a road

Example: The end of the street is blocked by a truck.

the extreme extent of something

Example: We did not leave until the very end.

the last part of something

Example: His office is the room at the other end of the corridor.

energy /ˈɛnɚdʒi/

capacity for intense activity

Example: She's always full of energy.

the capacity to do work and overcome resistance

Example: She has the drive and the energy to complete the exercise.

source of power such as electricity

Example: It does not take much to improve your home's energy efficiency.

engine /ˈɛndʒɪn/

any machine designed to convert energy into mechanical work

Example: I got in the car and started the engine.

entertainment /ˌɛntɚˈteɪnmənt/

enjoyment and interest

Example: There will be live entertainment at the party.

enthusiasm /ɛnˈθuːziˌæzəm/

ardent or lively interest or eagerness

Example: Her voice was full of enthusiasm.

something that you are very interested in and spend a lot of time doing

Example: Reading is one of her many enthusiasms.

entry /ˈɛntɹi/

something, such as a door or gate, through which it is possible to enter a place

Example: The children were surprised by the sudden entry of their teacher.

the act of joining an organization or group

Example: It is extremely difficult for new companies to gain entry into the market.

something submitted to win a competition

Example: *Entry is open to anyone over the age of 18.*

environment /ɛnvˈaɪɹənmənt/

the external conditions or surroundings in which people live

Example: *The government should do more to protect the environment.*

the conditions in which a person, animal or plant lives or operates or in which an activity takes place

Example: *Hospitals have a duty to provide a safe working environment for all staff.*

the natural world of air, sea, land, plants, and animals

Example: *We're not doing enough to protect the environment from pollution.*

equipment /ɪkwˈɪpmənt/

a set of devices or tools used for a particular purpose

Example: *The photographer came early to set up his equipment.*

error /ˈɛɹɚ/

a mistake, inaccuracy, or misjudgment

Example: *There is no room for error in this job.*

establishment /ɪstˈæblɪʃmənt/

the act of establishing or the state of being established

Example: *The speaker announced the establishment of a new college.*

a business organization or other institution

Example: *The hotel is a comfortable and well-run establishment.*

estate /ɪstˈeɪt/

a large piece of landed property

Example: *The family has a large estate in the countryside.*

a large area of land with houses or factories built on it

Example: *She receives rent from all the people whose houses are on estate land.*

property or possessions, especially of a deceased person
Example: Her estate was left to her daughter.

event /ɪv'ɛnt/
a planned and organized occasion
Example: They were invited to attend the social event of the year.
a thing that happens, especially something important
Example: Everyone was frightened by the strange sequence of events.

exam /ɛgz'æm/
the act of examining
Example: I went to the hospital to get an eye exam.
exercises, questions, or tasks set to test a person's knowledge and skills
Example: I got my exam results today.

examination /ɛgzˌæmɪn'eɪʃən/
the act of examining
Example: An athlete, for example, might turn the pedals 80 times a minute.
exercises, questions, or tasks set to test a person's knowledge and skills
Example: The students will write their examination in the auditorium.

Example /ɛgz'æmpəl/
a specimen that is typical of its group
Example: This is a good example of the artist's early work.
a particular event, object, or person that demonstrates a point or supports an argument
Example: It is possible to combine computer science with other subjects, for example, physics.
a person, action, or thing that is worthy of imitation
Example: Her courage is an example to us all.
to punish somebody as a warning to others not to do the same thing
Example: The teacher made an example of him by suspending him from school.

exchange /ɛkstʃˈeɪndʒ/

anything given or received as an equivalent or substitute for something else

Example: The exchange of prisoners took place this morning.

an argument

Example: There was only time for a brief exchange.

arrangement when two people or groups from different countries visit each other's homes or do each other's jobs for a short time.

Example: The exchange student from France will arrive soon.

excitement /ɛksˈaɪtmənt/

the state of being excited

Example: The news caused great excitement among her friends.

exercise /ˈɛksɚsˌaɪz/

physical exertion, especially for training or keeping fit

Example: Swimming is good exercise.

an activity planned to achieve a particular purpose

Example: I want you to do the next exercise in the book.

experience /ɛkspˈiəɹɪəns/

direct personal participation or observation of something

Example: The new player will bring a wealth of experience to the team.

a particular event that a person has undergone

Example: Experience has taught me that life can be very unfair.

the accumulated knowledge of practical matters

Example: My lack of practical experience was a disadvantage.

explanation /ɛksplɛnˈeɪʃən/

the reason or reasons why a particular event or situation happened

Example: She did not give an adequate explanation for being late.

expression /ɛkspɹˈɛʃən/

the transforming of ideas into words

Example: He describes drawing as a very personal form of artistic expression.

a showing of emotions without words

Example: The expression on her face is priceless.

extent /ɛkstˈɛnt/

the length, area, or size of something

Example: You cannot see the full extent of the beach from here.

the seriousness of a situation or difficulty

Example: It is difficult to assess the full extent of the damage.

eye /ˈaɪ/

the organ of sight in humans and animals

Example: I have something in my eye.

attention or observation

Example: A surgeon needs a good eye and a steady hand.

a small hole, such as the one at the blunt end of a sewing needle

Example: The thread was too thick for the eye of the needle.

a small area of calm in the centre of a storm, hurricane, or tornado

Example: They were in the eye of the storm.

Ff

face /fˈeɪs/
the front of the head from the forehead to the lower jaw
Example: *She has a long, thin face.*
the front or main side of an object, building, etc.
Example: *A banner hung across the face of the building.*
the surface of a clock or watch that has the numbers or hands on it
Example: *The clock has a very large face!*

fact /fˈɑkt/
an event or thing known to have happened or existed
Example: *The judge instructed both lawyers to stick to the facts of the case.*
a truth that can be proved from experience or observation
Example: *The story is based on fact.*

failure /fˈeɪlɪr/
the act of failing
Example: *All my efforts ended in failure.*
someone or something that is unsuccessful
Example: *The whole thing was a complete failure.*
the fact of something required or expected is not being done or not happening
Example: *Failure to comply with the rules will lead to serious consequences.*

fall /fˈɔːl/
an act of falling
Example: *I had a bad fall and broke my arm.*

fame /fˈeɪm/
the state of being widely known or recognized

Example: He gained fame as an actor.

family /fˈæmɪli/
a social group consisting of parents and their offspring
Example: A new family moved in next door.
all the people living together in one household
Example: The family lived beside the public road.
a large group of related types of animals or plants
Example: The lion is a member of the cat family.

fan /fˈɑn/
any device for creating a current of air, especially a rotating machine of blades attached to a central hub
Example: The breeze from the electric fan was very cold.
a person who admires or is enthusiastic about a someone or something, such as a pop star, actor, hobby, pastime, etc.
Example: Crowds of football fans filled the streets.

farmer /fˈɑːrmɚ/
a person who owns or manages a farm
Example: The farmer is picking the fruits from the tree.

fat fˈɑt/
extra or unwanted flesh on the body
Example: I could eat what I liked without getting fat.
a greasy or oily substance obtained from
animals or plants and used in cooking
Example: This product contains no animal fat.

feature /fˈiːtʃɚ/
a prominent or distinctive part of something
Example: An interesting feature of the city is the old market.
the main film in a cinema programme
Example: The programme had a special feature on education.

a part of somebody's face such as their nose, mouth, and eyes

Example: Her eyes are her most striking feature.

feedback /fˈiːdbɑk/

information in response to an inquiry or experiment

Example: The teacher will give you feedback on the test.

the return of part of the sound output of a loudspeaker to the microphone, so that a high-pitched whine is produced

Example: We were getting some feedback from the microphone.

feet /fˈiːt/

the part of the leg below the ankle joint that is in contact with the ground during standing and walking

Example: He was wearing boots on his feet.

a unit of measurement

Example: He is six feet tall.

feminism /ˈfɛmɪˌnɪzəm/

a doctrine or movement that advocates equal rights for women.

Example: She hosted a meeting on the future of feminism.

field /fˈiːld/

an area of uncultivated grassland

Example: We had to walk across a ploughed field.

a marked-off area on which sports or athletic competitions are held

Example: Every player on the field did their best today.

a particular subject or activity that somebody works in or is interested in

Example: He was awarded a Nobel Prize for his work in this field.

figure /fˈɪɡjɚ/

a written symbol for a number

Example: Her salary is now in six figures.

an amount expressed in numbers

Example: Her argument is backed up with plenty of facts and figures.

film /fˈɪlm/

a sequence of images projected onto a screen, creating the illusion of movement

Example: We're going out to see a film.

a thin sheet of any material, as of plastic for packaging

Example: There was no film in the camera.

finding /fˈaɪndɪŋ/

the conclusion reached after an inquiry or investigation

Example: This result confirms the findings of many previous studies.

fire /fˈaɪɚ/

the state of combustion producing heat, flames, and often smoke

Example: Most animals are afraid of fire.

the act of shooting weapons

Example: The gunmen opened fire on the police.

passion and enthusiasm

Example: Her eyes were full of fire.

firework /fˈaɪɚwɜːk/

a device containing chemicals that are ignited to produce coloured sparks and sometimes bangs

Example: They set off fireworks in the backyard.

fish /fˈɪʃ/

a cold-blooded animal with a backbone, gills, and usually fins and a skin covered in scales

Example: The fish swam quickly in the pond.

flag /flˈɑg/

a piece of cloth often attached to a pole used as an emblem or for signaling

Example: The black and white flag went down, and the race began.

a code inserted into a computer file to distinguish certain information

Example: He placed a flag on the program.

flight /flˈaɪt/

a journey by aircraft

Example: *Flight was still an exciting adventure for him.*

a set of stairs between one landing and the next

Example: *She fell down a flight of stairs and hurt her back.*

the act of running away, especially from danger

Example: *His flight was an indication of his guilt.*

flock /flˈɔːk/

a group of animals of one kind especially sheep and birds

Example: *A flock of birds flew over my house.*

a large group of people, especially of the same type

Example: *A noisy flock of tourists came into the building.*

waste from fabrics such as cotton or wool, used for stuffing mattresses

Example: *The pillow was filled with flock.*

focus /fˈoʊkəs/

a point of convergence of light or sound waves, or a point from which they appear to diverge

Example: *The heat of sunlight at the focus of a magnifying glass can easily set dry leaves on fire.*

a point upon which attention or activity is concentrated

Example: *It was the focus of attention at the meeting.*

the point at which an earthquake starts to happen

Example: *The earthquake's focus was at exactly 37 degrees north, 18 degrees south 75 meters below the ground.*

a point or distance at which the outline of an object is clearly seen by the eye or through a lens

Example: *The binoculars were not in focus*

food /fˈuːd/

any substance that can be taken into the body by a living organism and changed into energy and body tissue

Example: The store specializes in frozen foods.

foot /fʊt/

the part of the leg below the ankle joint that is in contact with the ground during standing and walking

Example: She kicked the ball with her right foot.

a unit for measuring length equal to 12 inches or 30.48 centimetres

Example: We had over a foot of snow in a few hours.

football /fʊtbɔːl/

any of various games played with a ball in which two teams compete to kick, or propel the ball into each other's goal

Example: The children were outside playing football.

the ball used in any of these games

Example: He kicked the football into the yard.

footprint /fʊtprɪnt/

an indentation or outline of the foot on a surface

Example: He could identify any animal from its footprints.

force /fɔːrs/

exertion or the use of exertion against a person or thing that resists

Example: The protestors were taken away by force.

an influence that changes a body from a state of rest to one of motion or changes its rate of motion

Example: You must apply some force to move the lever.

a group of people organized for particular duties or tasks

Example: The Police force was praised for reducing crime in the city.

form /fɔːrm/

the shape or appearance of something

Example: They made out a shadowy form in front of them.

the particular mode in which a thing or person appears

Example: The disease can take several different forms.

a type or kind

Example: *Swimming is one of the best forms of exercise.*

a printed document

Example: *I filled out a form on their website.*

fortune /fˈɔːrtʃʊn/

a person's destiny

Example: *She can tell your fortune by looking at the lines on your hand.*

wealth or material prosperity

Example: *He made a fortune in real estate.*

foundation /faʊndˈeɪʃən/

the basic experience, idea, or attitude on which a way of life or belief is based

Example: *Respect and friendship provide a solid foundation for marriage.*

a construction below the ground that distributes the load of a building, wall, etc.

Example: *The builders are now beginning to lay the foundations of the new school*

an endowment for the support of an institution, such as a university

Example: *The money will go to the new AIDS Foundation.*

the act of starting a new institution or organization

Example: *The organization has grown enormously since its foundation in 1955.*

frame /frˈeɪm/

a strong border or structure of wood, metal, etc. that holds a picture, door, piece of glass, etc. in position

Example: *She leaned against the frame of the door.*

the supporting structure of a piece of furniture, a building, a vehicle, etc. that gives it its shape

Example: *The bed frame is made of pine.*

a structure of plastic or metal that holds the lenses in a pair of glasses

Example: The spectacle frame is very expensive.

freedom /frˈiːdəm/
the state of being free
Example: He finally won his freedom after twenty years in jail.
the right or privilege of unrestricted access
Example: I was given the freedom to do anything I want.
the power or right to do or say what you want without anyone stopping you
Example: Everyone has the right to freedom of expression.
exemption or immunity
Example: All people should be guaranteed freedom from fear.

freezer /frˈiːzɚ/
an insulated cabinet for cold storage of perishable foods
Example: I always keep the meat in the freezer

friendship /frˈɛndʃɪp/
the emotions or conduct of friends; the state of being friends
Example: I value her friendship above anything else.

frog /frˈɔːg/
a smooth-skinned tailless amphibian with long back legs used for jumping
Example: The frog jumped into the pond.
an ornamental braiding for fastening the front of a garment that consists of a button and a loop through which it passes
Example: The frog is a flame-resistant clothing developed for the US Marine.
an organ on the bottom of a horse's hoof that assists in the circulation of blood
Example: The frog is a very important part of a horse's hoof.

fun /fˈʌn/
pleasant, enjoyable, and light-hearted activity or amusement
Example: We had a lot of fun at the party.

funeral /fjˈuːnə-rəl/

a ceremony at which a dead person is buried or cremated

Example: Hundreds of people attended his funeral.

future /fjˈuːtʃə-/

the time yet to come

Example: Nobody can predict the future.

the condition of a person or thing at a later date

Example: The company faces a very uncertain future.

Gg

gallows /gˈaloʊz/

a wooden structure consisting of two upright posts with a crossbeam, used for hanging criminals

Example: He was sentenced to death on the gallows.

game /gˈeɪm/

an amusement for children

Example: I play online games with my friends.

a competitive activity with rules

Example: The adults were playing a game of chess.

gang /gˈaŋ/

a group of people who go around together, often to commit crime

Example: Several gang members have been arrested.

an organized group of workmen

Example: A gang of labourers quickly cleared the field.

a group of young people who spend a lot of time together and often cause trouble or fight against other groups

Example: We were all in the same gang.

garbage /gˈɑːrbɪdʒ/

household waste

Example: The Park was littered with garbage.

worthless rubbish or nonsense

Example: Do not listen to the garbage that comes out of his mouth.

a container where people put things that are being thrown out

Example: Throw the can in the garbage.

garden /gˈɑːrdən/

an area of land usually next to a house, for growing flowers, fruits, or vegetables

Example: We planted a small garden in our backyard.

gate /gˈeɪt/

a movable barrier, usually hinged, for closing an opening in a wall or fence

Example: Students were still standing outside the school gate.

an exit at an airport by which passengers get to an aircraft

Example: All passengers for Paris should proceed to gate 8.

geese /gˈiːs/

the plural of goose; a fairly large web-footed long-necked migratory bird

Example: The geese flew into the pond.

gene /dʒˈiːn/

a unit composed of DNA forming part of a chromosome, by which inherited characteristics are transmitted from parent to offspring

Example: She inherited a good set of genes from her parents.

genus /dʒˈɛnəs/

one of the groups into which a family is divided, containing one or more species

Example: Members of this genus of beetles are typically flightless.

giant /dʒˈaɪənt/

a mythical figure of superhuman size and strength

Example: The giant destroyed the city.

something unusually large or powerful

Example: The Great Pyramids of Egypt are giants *among the world's architectural wonders.*

gift /gˈɪft/

something given to someone

Example: The watch was a gift from my mother.

a special ability or power

Example: He has a gift for making friends easily.

girl /gˈʌrl/

a female child; a young woman

Example: The little girl is skipping outside.

girlfriend /gˈʌrlfrɛnd/

any female friend

Example: Mary and her girlfriend organized the party.

a female friend with whom a person is romantically involved

Example: His girlfriend will be coming today.

glass /glˈæs/

a hard brittle transparent solid, consisting of metal silicates or similar compounds

Example: I cut myself on a piece of broken glass.

a drinking vessel made of glass

Example: He poured orange juice into a glass.

goal /gˈoʊl/

the space into which players try to propel the ball or puck to score

Example: The player kicked the ball into the goal.

an aim or purpose

Example: Their primary goal is to make a profit.

goat /gˈoʊt/

an agile cud-chewing mammal with hollow horns

Example: The goat ate all the vegetables in the garden.

golf /gˈɔːlf/

a game in which a ball is struck with clubs into a series of eighteen holes in a grassy course

Example: I play golf every weekend.

goose /gˈuːs/

a fairly large web-footed long-necked migratory bird; the female of such a bird

Example: The goose laid her eggs in the bushes.

government /gˈʌvə-nmənt/

the executive policy-making body of a country or state

Example: *The minister has announced that there will be no change in government policy.*

grandfather /grˈændfɑːðə-/

the father of one's father or mother

Example: *My grandfather is a great storyteller.*

grandmother /grˈændmʌðə-/

the mother of one's father or mother

Example: *We went to visit our grandmother in the hospital.*

grass /grˈæs/

a very common green plant with jointed stems and long narrow leaves, eaten by animals such as sheep and cows, and used for lawns and sports fields

Example: *The cows love to eat fresh green grass.*

greenhouse /grˈiːnhaʊs/

a building with glass walls and roof where plants are grown under controlled conditions.

Example: *George grows a lot of tomatoes in his greenhouse.*

grocery /grˈoʊsə-ri/

the business or premises of a grocer

Example: *I was carrying three heavy bags of groceries.*

group /grˈuːp/

a number of people or things considered as a unit

Example: *I am meeting a group of friends for dinner tonight.*

an association of business firms that have the same owner

Example: The Burton group announced its quarterly figures yesterday.

a number of people who work or do something together or share particular beliefs

Example: The residents formed a community action group.

growth /grˈoʊθ/

the process of growing

Example: Lack of water will stunt the plant's growth.

an increase e in size, number, or significance

Example: The report links population growth with rural poverty.

any abnormal tissue, such as a tumor

Example: He had a cancerous growth on his lung.

guest /gˈɛst/

a person who receives hospitality at someone else's home

Example: She had invited six guests to dinner.

a person who is taken out socially by someone else who pays all the expenses

Example: They only use the dining room when they have guests.

a performer or speaker taking part in an event, show, or film by special invitation

Example: He was invited as a guest speaker.

a person who is staying in a hotel

Example: We have accommodation for 500 guests.

guidance /gˈaɪdəns/

help, advice, or instruction, usually from someone more experienced or more qualified

Example: The helpline was set up for young people in need of guidance and support.

guide /gˈaɪd/

a person who conducts parties of tourists around places of interest, such as museums

Example: *Our tour guide showed us around the old town.*

something that can be used to gauge something or to help in planning one's actions

Example: *His elder sister had been his guide, counsellor and friend.*

a member of an organization for girls that encourages discipline and practical skills

Example: *The members of the girl's guide were responsible for selling cookies in the community.*

guitar /gɪtˈɑːr/

a stringed instrument with a flat back and a long neck with a fretted fingerboard, which is played by plucking or strumming

Example: *I am learning to play the guitar.*

Hh

hair /hˈɛr/
any of the threadlike outgrowths on the skin of mammals
Example: I am learning to play the guitar.
a very small distance or margin
Example: He won the race by a hair.

haircut /hˈɛrkʌt/
the style in which a person's hair is cut
Example: You need a haircut.

half /hˈɔf/
either of two equal or corresponding parts that together make up a whole
Example: The second half of the book is more exciting.
either of two periods of time into which a sports game, concert, etc. is divided
Example: She played well in the second half of the match.
Half past a particular hour is 30 minutes later than that hour
Example: I will meet you at half past nine

hall /hˈɔːl/
an entry area into other rooms in a house
Example: I left my bags in the hall.
a building or room for public meetings, dances, etc.
Example: I am playing in a concert at the church hall.
a residential building in a college or university
Example: Students usually eat breakfast in the hall.

hallway /hˈɔːlweɪ/
a passageway or room between the entrance and the interior of a building
Example: He hurried them along the narrow, dark hallway.

halo /hˈeɪloʊ/

a ring of light around the head of a sacred figure

Example: She played the part of an angel, complete with wings and a halo.

a circle of refracted light around the sun or moon

Example: There is a halo around the moon.

hamburger /hˈambɜːgɚ/

a flat round of minced beef often served in a bread roll

Example: He ate a hamburger for lunch today.

hand /hˈand/

the part of the body at the end of the arm, consisting of a thumb, four fingers, and a palm

Example: You must hold my hand when we cross the road.

help with doing something that needs a lot of effort

Example: Would you like a hand carrying those bags?

handcuff /hˈandkʌf/

a linked pair of locking metal rings used for securing prisoners

Example: She was taken to the police station in handcuffs.

happiness /hˈapɪnəs/

the state of being happy

Example: She has brought us much happiness over the years.

hardware /hˈɑːrdwɛr/

metal tools or implements, especially cutlery or cooking utensils

Example: The hardware store was closed for the day.

the physical equipment used in a computer system

Example: The cost of computer hardware has risen over the years.

hart /hˈɑːrt/

the male of the deer, especially the red deer

Example: He noticed a hart walking across the road.

hat /hˈɑt/

a head covering, often with a brim, usually worn to give protection from the weather

Example: The child wore a colourful hat to school this morning.

hate /hˈeɪt/

intense dislike

Example: I really hate Monday mornings.

hatred /hˈeɪtrɪd/

intense dislike

Example: There was fear and hatred in his voice.

head /hˈɛd/

the upper or front part of the body that contains the brain, eyes, mouth, nose, and ears

Example: She turned her head to look at him.

a person's mind and mental abilities

Example: I sometimes wonder what goes on in that head of yours.

the most forward part of a thing

Example: They finished the season at the head of their league.

the position of leadership or command

Example: She resigned as head of the department.

the side of a coin that has a picture of the head of a person on it. It is used as one choice when a coin is tossed to decide something

Example: I called heads and it came down tails.

the most important seat at a table

Example: The President sat at the head of the table.

used to say how many animals of a particular type are on a farm, in a herd, etc.

Example: The shepherd has 200 heads of sheep.

health /hˈɛlθ/

the general condition of the body and mind

Example: *Smoking can seriously damage your health.*

the state of being bodily and mentally vigorous and free from disease

Example: *Rest and exercise restored her health.*

the work of providing medical services

Example*:* *The health minister will be visiting the hospital later today.*

heap /hˈiːp/

a pile of things lying one on top of another

Example: *His clothes lay in a heap on the floor.*

a lot of something

Example: *They have a heap of time before the plane leaves.*

hearing /hˈaɪrɪŋ)

the sense by which sound is perceived

Example: *The explosion damaged his hearing.*

an official meeting at which the facts about a crime, complaint, etc. are presented to the person or group of people who will have to decide what action to take

Example: *An appeal hearing is scheduled for later this month.*

heart /hˈɑːrt/

a hollow muscular organ whose contractions pump blood throughout the body.

Example: *The patient's heart stopped beating for a few seconds.*

tenderness or pity

Example: *She has a kind heart.*

the most important part

Example: *The difference between right and wrong lies at the heart of all questions of morality.*

a thing that is like a heart in shape, often red and used as a symbol of love; a symbol like a heart used to mean the verb 'love'

Example: The words 'I love you' were written inside a big red heart.

heat /hˈiːt/

the state of being hot

Example: He could feel the heat of the sun on his back.

the level of temperature

Example: Test the heat of the water before getting in.

height /hˈaɪt/

the vertical distance from the bottom of something to the top

Example: The plant can reach a height of over six feet.

a particular distance above the ground

Example: The plane flew at a height of 3 000 metres.

heir /ˈɛr/

the person, male, legally succeeding to the property of a deceased person

*Example***:** The first prince is the heir to the throne.

heiress /ˈɛrɛs/

the person, female, legally succeeding to the property of a deceased person

Example: He adopts his niece as his heiress.

hen /hˈɛn/

the female of any bird, especially the domestic fowl

Example: The hen pecked a hole in the sack.

herd /hˈɜːd/

a large group of mammals, especially cattle, living and feeding together

Example: A herd of cattle had strayed onto the road.

a large group of people that is considered together as a group and not separately

Example: A herd of shoppers waited anxiously for the store to open.

hero /hˈɪəroʊ/

the principal male character in a novel, play, etc.

Example: The hero of the novel is a ten-year-old boy.

a man of exceptional courage, nobility, etc.

Example: He was hailed as a hero after the rescue.

heroine /hˈɛroʊˌɪn/

the principal female character in a novel, play, etc.

Example: The heroine in the story finally found true love.

a woman of exceptional courage, nobility, etc.

Example: The town remembered her as the heroine of the flood and erected a statue in her honor.

highway /hˈaɪweɪ/

a public road that everyone may use

Example: A parked car was obstructing the traffic on the highway.

historian /hɪstˈɔːriən/

a person who writes or studies history

Example: She is a writer as well as a distinguished modern historian.

history /hˈɪstɚri/

a record or account of past events and developments

Example: Many people throughout history have dreamt of a world without war.

the study of past events, especially as a subject at school or university

Example: I studied modern European history at university.

holiday /hˈɑːlɪdˌeɪ/

a period of time spent away from home for enjoyment and relaxation

Example: We went on holiday together last summer.

a day on which work is suspended by law or custom

Example: The president's birthday was declared a national holiday.

home /hˈoʊm/

the place where one lives

Example:　　She leaves home at 7 every day.

the country or area of one's birth

Example:　　I often think about my friends back home.

a building or organization set up to care for people in a certain category, such as orphans or the aged

Example:　　She had lived in an old people's home for the past ten years.

a place where something is invented or started

Example:　　Greece is known as the home of democracy.

homework /hˈoʊmwɜːk/

school work done at home

Example:　　I always do my homework in the classroom.

honesty /ˈɔnəsti/

the quality of being truthful and trustworthy

Example:　　She answered all my questions with her usual honesty.

honey /hˈʌni/

a sweet edible sticky substance made by bees from the nectar

Example:　　I bought a bottle of honey at the supermarket.

hoof /hˈuːf/

the horny covering of the end of the foot in the horse, deer, and certain other mammals

Example:　　The horse turned its head and stamped its hoof.

hope /hˈoʊp/

a feeling of desire for something, usually with confidence in the possibility of its fulfilment

Example:　　All we can do is wait and hope.

horse /ˈhɔrs/

a four-footed mammal with hooves, a mane, and a tail, used for riding and pulling carts

Example: He mounted his horse and rode off.

horsefly /ˈhɔːrsflaɪ/

a large fly which sucks the blood of horses, cattle, and people

Example: The little boy caught the horsefly that was bothering the horse for a long time.

hose /ˈhoʊz/

a flexible pipe, for conveying a liquid or gas

Example: There is a very long garden hose in the shed.

hospice /ˈhɔspəs/

a nursing home that specializes in caring for the terminally ill

Example: She founded an AIDS hospice with the help of a local doctor.

hospital /hˈɔːspɪtəl/

an institution for the medical or psychiatric care and treatment of patients

Example: I am going to the hospital to visit my brother.

host /ˈhoʊst/

a person who receives or entertains guests, especially in his own home

Example: We were greeted at the front door by our host.

the organization or country providing the facilities for a function or event

Example: Each year, the city plays host to the film festival for one week.

a person who talks to guests on a television or radio show

Example: He is the host of the talk show.

hostess /hˈoʊstɛs/

a woman who receives and entertains guests, especially in her own house

Example: We were greeted by our hostess.

a woman who talks to guests on a television or radio show

Example: She's the hostess of a popular talk show.

hotel /hoʊtˈɛl/

a commercially run establishment providing lodging and meals for guests
Example: We stayed in a friendly hotel for our vacation.

hotelier /hoʊˈtɛljɚ/
an owner or manager of a hotel
Example: She is the most successful hotelier in the country.

house /hˈaʊs/
a building used as a home
Example: We live in a two-bedroom house.

house arrest /ˈhaʊs ɚˈɛst/
confinement to one's own home rather than in prison
Example: The opposition leader has just been placed under house arrest.

houseboat /hˈaʊsboʊt/
a stationary boat used as a home
Example: They have been living on a houseboat for the past twelve years.

housecoat /ˈhaʊs ˈkoʊt/
a woman's loose robe-like garment for casual wear
Example: She was lying on the mat with her best housecoat.

housefly /ˈhaʊs ˈflaɪ/
a common fly often found in houses
Example: There's a housefly crawling along the wall!

household /ˈhaʊsˌhoʊɫd/
all the people living together in one house
Example: Most households now own at least one car.

housekeeper /ˈhaʊˌskipɚ/

a person employed to run someone else's household

Example: She has been a housekeeper at the Hall for many years.

houseman /ˈhaʊsmən/

a junior doctor in a hospital

Example: The houseman attended to his wounds.

housewife /ˈhaʊˌswaɪf/

a woman who runs her own household and does not have a paid job

Example: His father is a businessman while his mother is a housewife.

housework /ˈhaʊˌswɜːk/

the work of running a home, such as cleaning, cooking, and shopping

Example: He forgot his homework on the bus this morning.

housing /ˈhaʊzɪŋ/

the job of providing people with accommodation

Example: There is an urgent need to build more affordable housing.

houses collectively

Example: The city is building new housing for the elderly.

a case or covering that surrounds a machine or part of a machine

Example: The engine appeared to be intact except for the loss of its housing.

hovel /ˈhəvəl/

a small house or hut that is dirty or badly in need of repair

Example: Your house is a miserable hovel compared to my palace.

hovercraft /ˈhʌvɚˌkræft/

a vehicle that is able to travel across both land and water on a cushion of air

Example: They have invented and developed the jet engine and the hovercraft.

hubris /ˈhjubrəs/

pride or arrogance

Example: He was punished for his hubris.

huckster /ˈhəkstɚ/

a person who uses aggressive methods of selling

Example: They tried to huckster red socks to me.

huddle /ˈhədəl/

a small group of people or things standing or lying close together

Example: We huddled together for warmth.

huff /ˈhʌf/

a passing mood or anger or resentment

Example: "The project is a complete waste of time," she huffed.

hulk /ˈhʌlk/

the body of an abandoned ship

Example: The ship's rusting hulk is still visible on the rocks.

a large person

Example: He's a hulk of a man.

hull /ˈhʌl/

the main body of a boat

Example: They climbed onto the upturned hull and waited to be rescued.

humanism /ˈhjuməˌnɪzəm/

the rejection of religion in favour of a belief in the advancement of humanity by its own efforts

Example: Humanism flourished during the last century.

humanity /hjuˈmænɪti/

the quality of being human

Example: He was found guilty of crimes against humanity.

the quality of being kind to people and animals by making sure that they do not suffer more than is necessary; the quality of being humane

Example: *The man was praised for his courage and humanity.*

hunger /hˈʌŋɚ/

a feeling of emptiness or weakness caused by lack of food

Example: *She was faint with hunger.*

hunter /hˈʌntɚ/

a person or animal that seeks out and kills or captures the game

Example: *The hunters followed the tracks of the deer for hours.*

a person who searches for something

Example: *My mother is a bargain-hunter for good prices*

husband /ˈhʌzbənd/

a woman's partner in marriage

Example: *Her husband is a very successful lawyer.*

husk /ˈhʌsk/

the outer covering of certain fruits and seeds

Example: *Brown rice has not had the husks removed.*

hutch /ˈhʌtʃ/

a cage for small animals

Example: *I fed the rabbit a carrot through the wire netting of its hutch.*

hybrid /ˈhaɪbrəd/

an animal or plant resulting from a cross between two different types of animals or plant

Example: *The animal looks like a hybrid of a zebra and a horse.*

a vehicle with an engine that uses both petrol and another type of energy, usually electricity

Example: *Most cars manufacturers now offer hybrids.*

hydrant /ˈhaɪdrənt/

an outlet from a water main, from which water can be tapped for fighting fires

Example: The water poured from the sky as though a fire hydrant had been opened.

hydraulics /haɪˈdrɔlɪks/

the study of the mechanical properties of fluids as they apply to practical engineering

Example: The hydraulics failed, and the digger stopped.

hydride /ˈhaɪˌdraɪd/

a compound of hydrogen with another element

Example: The car can go up to 47 miles per hour on its nickel-metal hydride battery pack.

hydrocarbon /ˌhaɪdroʊˈkɑrbən/

a compound containing only carbon and hydrogen

Example: Oil, a liquid hydrocarbon, is a more neutral fuel.

hydrocephalus /ˌhaɪdroʊˈsɛfələs/

accumulation of fluid in the cavities of the brain, causing enlargement of the head in children

Example: He suffered from hydrocephalus.

hydrodynamics /ˈhaɪˌdroʊ daɪˈnæmɪks/

the branch of science concerned with the mechanical properties of fluids

Example: His research in hydrodynamics was highly useful for marine engineering.

hydrogen /hˈaɪdrədʒən/

a colourless gas that burns easily and is the lightest element in the universe

Example: The gas contains a certain amount of hydrogen and

hydrograph /ˈhaɪˌdroʊˈɡræf/

a graph showing variations in the amount of water in a river over a period of time

Example: They used the hydrograph to monitor the water in the nearby river.

hygiene /ˈhaɪˌdʒin/

the principles and practices of health and cleanliness

Example: Many skin diseases can be prevented by good personal hygiene.

hyperbole /haɪˈpɝbəˌli/

a deliberate exaggeration of speech or writing used for effect

Example: The film is being promoted with all the usual hyperbole.

hyperlink /ˈhaɪpɝˌlɪŋk/

a link from a hypertext file that gives users instant access to related material in another file

Example: She accidentally clicked on the hyperlink.

hypertext /ˈhaɪpɝˌtɛkst/

computer software and hardware that allows users to store and view text and move between related items easily

Example: The Web is based on hypertext links that allow people to easily move from document to document.

hypertrophy /ˈhaɪpɝˌtroʊfi/

enlargement of an organ or part resulting from an increase in the size of the cells

Example: Muscular hypertrophy is one of the signs of hypothyroidism.

hyperventilation /ˈhaɪpɝˌvɛnəˈłeɪʃən/

an increase in the rate of breathing at rest, sometimes resulting in cramps and dizziness

Example: Hyperventilation can be caused by fear or panic.

hyphen /ˈhaɪfən/

the punctuation mark (-) is used to separate parts of compound words and between syllables of a word split between two consecutive lines

Example: Is there a hyphen in post-mortem?

hypnosis /hɪpˈnoʊsəs/

an artificially induced state of relaxation in which the mind is more than usually receptive to suggestion

Example: Under deep hypnosis, she remembered the traumatic events of that night.

hypochondria /ˌhaɪpəˈkɑndriə/

abnormal anxiety concerning one's health

Example: I thought the doctor was going to accuse me of hypochondria.

hypocrisy /hɪˈpɑkrəsi/

the practice of claiming to have standards or beliefs that are contrary to one's a real character or actual behavior

Example: He condemned the hypocrisy of those politicians who do one thing and say another.

hypocrite /ˈhɪpəˌkrɪt/

a person who pretends to be what he or she is not

Example: Charles was a liar and a hypocrite who married her for money.

hypotension /ˌhaɪpoʊˈtɛnʃən/

abnormally low blood pressure

Example: He has always suffered from hypertension.

hypothermia /ˌhaɪpəˈθɜrmiə/

an abnormally low body temperature, as a result of exposure to cold

Example: Many elderly people are dying needlessly because of hypothermia.

hypothesis /haɪˈpɑθəsəs/

a suggested explanation for a group of facts accepted either as a basis for further verification or as likely to be true

Example: There is little evidence to support these hypotheses.

hysterectomy /ˌhɪstɚˈɛktəmi/

surgical removal of the womb

Example: She had to have a hysterectomy.

hysteria /hɪˈstɛriə/

a mental disorder marked by emotional outbursts and, often, symptoms such as paralysis

Example: There was mass hysteria when the singer came on stage.

hysterics /ˌhɪsˈtɛrɪks/

an attack of hysteria

Example: He went into hysterics when he heard the news.

Ii

ibis /ˈaɪbəs/

a large wading bird with a long thin curved bill

Example: Twenty feet in front of us, a white ibis, hunting in the shallows with its long-curved bill, squawked and took flight, fluttering out of sight.

ice /ˈaɪs/

water that has frozen and becomes solid

Example: The ice melted quickly in the sun.

iceberg /ˈaɪsbɚg/

a large mass of ice floating in the sea.

Example: A brilliant doctor, but both patients and staff complain that he is an iceberg.

icebreaker /ˈaɪsˌbreɪkɚ/

a ship designed to move through ice

Example: Many icebreaker ships use nuclear marine propulsion.

a game or joke that makes people who do not know each other feel more relaxed together.

Example: I encourage my students to use icebreakers to get to know each other.

icicle /ˈaɪsɪkəl/

a tapering spike of ice hanging where water has dripped

Example: A long-pointed stick of ice is formed when drops of water freeze.

icing /ˈaɪsɪŋ/

a mixture of sugar and water or egg whites used to cover and decorate cakes

Example: This cake is a rich baked fruit cake with icing and sugar frosting.

iconoclast /ˌaɪˈkɑnəˌklæst/

a person who attacks established or traditional ideas or principles

Example: He is an iconoclast, working stiff; a company man, and a virtuoso.

id /ˈɪd/

the primitive instincts and energies in the unconscious mind that underlie all psychological impulses

Example: The id is responsible for his portrayal of bad behaviour.

idea /aɪˈiə/

any product of mental activity; thought

Example: Do you have any idea of what he looks like?

ideal /aɪˈdil/

a conception of something that is perfect

Example: In an ideal world no one would go hungry.

idealism /aɪˈdiɑlɪzəm/

belief in or striving towards ideals

Example: She never lost her youthful idealism and campaigned for just causes all her life.

identity /aɪˈdɛntɪˌti/

the state of being a specified person or thing

Example: The man's identity was being kept secret while he was helping police with their investigation.

idiom /ˈɪdiəm/

a group of words that, when used together, have a different meaning from the one suggested by the individual words

Example: I was not familiar with the idiom, so I had to guess what he meant.

idiot /ˈɪˌdiət/

a foolish or senseless person

Example: Some idiot left the faucet running in the bathroom and there's water everywhere.

idol /ˈaɪdəl/

an object of excessive devotion or admiration

Example: In many systems of belief. Idols have symbolic value.

idolatry /aɪˈdɑlətri/

the worship of idols

Example: The youngster makes no attempt to conceal the idolatry of his team-mate.

ignition /ˌɪgˈnɪʃən/

the system used to ignite the fuel in an internal-combustion engine

Example: An engine's ignition is the electrical system that starts the engine.

ignoramus /ˌɪgnɚˈeɪməs/
an ignorant person
Example: I am a complete ignoramus where computers are concerned.

ignorance /ˈɪgnɚəns/
lack of knowledge or education
Example: I am embarrassed by my complete ignorance of history.

iguana /ɪgjuːˈɑːnɐ/
a large tropical tree lizard of the West Indies and South America with a spiny back
Example: An iguana is a type of large lizard found in America.

illness /ˈɪlnəs/
a disease or indisposition
Example: He died after a long illness.

illumination /ɪˌluməˈneɪʃən/
a source of light
Example: Higher levels of illumination are needed for reading.

illusion /ˌɪˈluʒən/
a false appearance or deceptive impression of reality
Example: No one really has any illusions about winning the war.

illustration /ˌɪləˈstreɪʃən/
a picture or diagram used to explain or decorate a text
Example: An illustration in a book is a picture, design, or diagram.

imagery/ˈɪmədʒri/
the figurative or descriptive language in a literary work
Example: The nature imagery of the ballad is quite striking.

image /ˈɪmɪdʒ/

a mental picture of someone or something produced by the imagination or memory

Example: She had an image in her mind even before she met her new boss.

imagination /ɪmˌædʒɪnˈeɪʃən/

the faculty or action of producing mental images of what is not present or in one's experience

Example: Antonia is a woman with a vivid imagination.

imbalance /ɪmˈbæləns/

a lack of balance, for instance in proportion or emphasis

Example: The imbalance between the two sides in this war.

imbroglio /ˌɪmˈbroʊlˌjoʊ/

a confusing and complicated situation

Example: She did not appear amused to be pulled into his imbroglio.

imitation /ˌɪməˈteɪʃən/

a copy of an original or genuine article

Example: This latest production is a pale imitation of the original.

behaviour modelled on the behaviour of someone else

Example: An imitation of something is a copy of it.

immigrant /ˈɪməgrənt/

a person who comes to a foreign country in order to settle there

Example: They are immigrants from a very poor country.

the act of coming to a foreign country in order to settle there

Example: The government has decided to tighten its immigration policy.

immunity /ˌɪmˈjunəti/

the ability of an organism to resist disease

Example: He was not old enough to have developed immunity to it yet.

immunodeficiency /ˌɪmjunoʊdɪˈfɪʃənsi/

a deficiency in or breakdown of a person's ability to fight diseases

Example: It forms a constituent of the human immunodeficiency virus lipodystrophy syndrome.

immunology /ˌɪmjuˈnɔlədʒi/

the branch of medicine concerned with the study of immunity

Example: She was a founding member of the immunology division.

impact /ˈɪmpækt/

the effect or impression made by something

Example: The shock of diagnosis can have a huge impact on someone.

impasse /ˈɪmˌpæs/

a situation in which progress or escape is impossible

Example: The proposal offered both sides a way out of the diplomatic impasse.

impediment /ˌɪmˈpɛdəmənt/

a hindrance or obstruction

Example: I had a bad speech impediment.

a physical disability that makes speech or walking difficult

Example: It is often presumed that the speech impediment is caused by shyness.

imperfection /ˌɪmpɚˈfɛkʃən/

the state of being imperfect

Example: They learned to live with each other's imperfections.

implication /ˌɪmpləˈkeɪʃən/

something that is suggested or implied

Example: We looked at the implications for the wild population.

importance /ɪmpˈoːrtəns/

the state or fact of being of great significance or value

Example: Do they know the importance of food for concentration?

imposition /ˌɪmpəˈzɪʃən/

the act of imposing

Example: The preferred policy has, so far, been the imposition of sanctions.

impossibility /ˌɪmˌpɑsɪˈbɪlɪti/

the state or quality of being impossible

Example: She finally acknowledged the impossibility of keeping her boyfriend's secret.

imposter /ˌɪmˈpɔstɚ/

a person who cheats or swindles by pretending to be someone else

Example: He could be an impostor.

impression /ɪmprˈɛʃən/

an effect produced in the mind by a person or thing

Example: My first impression, was that the man was carrying him off.

a vague idea or belief.

Example: Yet that first impression of identity lingered on for Carol.

imprint /ˈɪmprɪnt/

a mark or impression produced by pressing, printing, or stamping

Example: Your physical flaws are imprinted in your mind.

impropriety /ˌɪmprəˈpraɪəti/

unsuitable or slightly improper behavior

Example: There has been no procedural impropriety.

improvement /ɪmprˈuːvmənt/

the act of improving or the state of being improved; to make better

Example: There are no recent signs of improvement.

improvisation /ˌɪmprɒvɪˈzeɪʃən/

the process of making something from whatever material is available

Example: The second big improvement is the support cast.

income /ˈɪŋkʌm/

the total amount of money earned from work or obtained from other sources over a given period of time.

Example: We are on a low income but just not quite low enough to be eligible for grants.

independence /ˌɪndɪpˈɛndəns/

the fact or state of being independent

Example: There will be a huge independence party this weekend.

index /ˈɪndɛks/

an alphabetical list of names or subjects dealt with in a book, indicating where they are referred to

Example: She converted to Catholicism and helped to index his many books.

a number or ratio indicating a specific characteristics or property

Example: She notes the index number but is one digit out.

indication /ˌɪndɪkˈeɪʃən/

a sign or piece of information that indicates something

Example: Helen's face gave no indication of what she was thinking.

industry /ˈɪndʌstri/

the work and process involved with the manufacture of a specified product

Example: The makeup industry is quite popular around the world.

the quality of working hard

Example: But the financial services industry slammed the ban.

inflation /ɪnfl'eɪʃən/

a progressive increase in the general level of prices brought about by an increase in the amount of money in circulation or by increases in costs

Example: Shoppers should beware of hidden inflation.

information /ˌɪnfɚm'eɪʃən/

knowledge acquired in any manner

Example: We should not have to search for this information elsewhere.

initiative /ɪn'ɪʃiətˌɪv/

a first step

Example: He also references an initiative involving employers.

injury /'ɪndʒɚri/

physical hurt

Example: That seems to be a serious injury.

damage

Example: Dozens of people suffered head injuries

innocence /'ɪnəsəns/

the quality or state of being innocent

Example: He also has a childlike innocence.

insanity /ɪns'æniti/

the state of being insane

Example: He suffered from periodic bouts of insanity.

insect /'ɪnsɛkt/

a small animal that has six legs and usually has wings, such as an ant, fly, or butterfly

Example: The defining feature of insects is that they have six legs.

inside /ɪns'aɪd/

the inner side, surface, or part of something

Example: He then went back inside the apartment and called the police.

inspection /ɪnspˈɛkʃən/

the act to examine closely, especially for faults or errors

Example: She arrived to carry out a health and safety inspection of the building.

inspector /ɪnspˈɛktɚ/

an official who checks that things or places meet certain regulations and standards

Example: He finally reached the rank of inspector.

instance /ˈɪnstəns/

a case or example

Example: There have been several instances of that happening.

instruction /ɪnstrˈʌkʃən/

a direction or order

Example: Read the instructions carefully because controls vary

insurance /ɪnʃˈʊrəns/

the agreement by which one makes regular payments to a company who pay an agreed sum if damage, loss, or death occurs

Example: The insurance company is more comfortable if the family moves in.

intelligence /ɪntˈɛlɪdʒəns/

the ability to understand, learn, and think things out quickly

Example: He did not even have the intelligence to call for an ambulance.

a group or department collecting military information

Example: German intelligence relies on both of those countries sharing information with it.

intention /ɪntˈɛnʃən/

a plan, idea, or purpose

Example: Eight men initially declared their intention to stand.

interaction /ˌɪntɚˈækʃən/

communication or direct involvement with someone or something

Example: He suggests that we all should focus more on face-to-face interaction.

interest /ˈɪntrɛst/

curiosity or concern about someone or something

Example: Her work reflects her interest in social and cultural systems.

money paid for the use of credit or borrowed money

Example: They had little interest in balanced findings.

a group of people with common aims

Example: She finds it interesting to hear what I have to say.

internet /ˈɪntɚnˌɛt/

a large public-access computer network linked to others worldwide

Example: I bought my basketball tickets on the Internet.

introduction /ˌɪntrədˈʌkʃən/

the act of introducing something or someone

Example: Introductions were made, and the conversation started to flow.

the first part of a book or speech that gives a general idea of what is to follow

Example: Can you write a brief introduction to the text?

investment /ɪnvˈɛstmənt/

the act of investing money

Example: He says that investment in this field is crucial.

iron /ˈaɪən/

a strong silvery-white metallic element, widely used for structural and engineering purposes

Example: Iron rusts easily.

a small electrically heated device with a weighted flat bottom for pressing clothes

Example: Get others to iron their own shirts in the future.

issue /ˈɪʃuː/

a topic of interest or discussion

Example: The visa issue is a particular sticking point.

a particular edition of a magazine or journal

Example: There is an article on motorbikes in the latest issue.

item /ˈaɪtəm/

a single thing in a list or collection

Example: The restaurant has a long menu of about 50 items.

Jj

jack /ˈdʒak/

a mechanical device used to raise a motor vehicle or other heavy object

Example: You need a car jack to change a tire.

jacket /ˈdʒækət/

a short coat with a front opening and long sleeves

Example: I left my leather jacket in the car.

jackpot /ˈdʒak‚pɔt/

the most valuable prize that can be won in a gambling game

Example: The jackpot was over $1 million.

jacuzzi /dʒəˈkuzi/

a large circular bath with a mechanism that swirls the water

Example: Some of the amenities on board include an outside jacuzzi.

jade /ˈdʒeɪd/

an ornamental semiprecious stone, usually green in colour

Example: The ring has jade green flower heads which turn deep burgundy as they age.

jaguar /ˈdʒæˌgwɑr/

a large wild cat from South and Central America, with a spotted coat

Example: The yellow eyes of the jaguar shine brightly in the moonlight.

jail /ˈdʒeɪl/

a prison

Example: He was sentenced to six months in jail.

jam /dʒˈæm/

food made from fruit boiled with sugar until the mixture sets, used for spreading on bread

Example: I enjoy eating strawberry jam on toast.

jamb /ˈdʒɑm/

aside post of a doorframe or window frame

Example: The columns and door jambs are also painted.

janitor /ˈdʒænətɚ/

the caretaker of a school or other building

Example: The janitor was cleaning the windows and had temporarily left them open.

jar /ˈdʒɑr/

a wide-mouthed cylindrical glass container, used for storing food

Example: Both plants and herbs can be stored in opaque glass storage jars with tight-fitting lids.

jargon /ˈdʒɑrgən/

specialized language relating to a particular subject, profession, or group

Example: He'd culled enough jargon from his own victim research to make it look like the real thing, he thought.

jaundice /ˈdʒɔndəs/

yellowing of the skin and the whites of the eyes, caused by an excess of bile pigments in the blood

Example: Did your physician confirm the jaundice by a blood test?

jaunt /ˈdʒɔnt/

a pleasure trip or outing

Example: We let him back in after his little jaunt.

jaw /ˈdʒɔ/

either of the bones that hold the teeth and frame the mouth

Example: He has a strong square jaw

jazz /ˈdʒɑz/

a kind of popular music of African-American origin that has an exciting rhythm and often involves improvisation

Example: The renowned saxophonist plays contemporary jazz.

jealousy /ˈdʒɛləsi/

the state of or an instance of feeling jealous

Example: He's being driven by jealousy rather than love.

jelly /ˈdʒɛli/

a fruit-flavoured dessert set with gelatin

Example: Pour the custard over the trifle when the jelly is set.

jeopardy /ˈdʒɛpɚdi/

danger of harm, loss, or death

Example: His job was in jeopardy and the future seemed bleak.

jersey /ˈdʒɝzi/

a knitted garment covering the upper part of the body

Example: Put the red and blue jersey on.

jest /ˈdʒɛst/

something done or said to amuse people

Example: You can joke and jest all the time in the hotel.

jester /ˈdʒɛstɚ/

a professional clown employed by a king or nobleman during the Middle Ages

Example: I am a jester.

jet /ˈdʒɛt/

an aircraft driven by jet propulsion

Example: The jet stream is driven by the temperature difference at high altitudes between the polar region and the equator.

a thin stream of liquid or gas forced out of a small hole.

Example: The jet stream was also particularly strong and far south.

jewel /ˈdʒuəl/

a precious or semiprecious stone

Example: She wore a white blouse with gathered cuffs and jewels.

jeweler /ˈdʒuələ˞/

a person who buys, sells, and repairs jewelry

Example: She carried her jeweler's tools and supplies to her training.

jewellery /dʒˈuːəlri/

objects such as rings, necklaces, and bracelets, worn for decoration

Example: That chain looks like a piece of jewellery to me.

jigsaw /ˈdʒɪɡˌsɔ/

a puzzle in which the player has to put together a picture that has been cut into irregularly shaped interlocking pieces

Example: There are still two missing pieces of the jigsaw.

a mechanical saw with a fine steel blade for cutting along curved or irregular lines in sheets of material

Example: This felt like the final piece of the jigsaw.

jingle /ˈdʒɪŋgəl/

a short catchy song used to advertise a product on radio or television

Example: Its catchy jingle goes off suddenly.

jinx /ˈdʒɪŋks/

someone or something believed to bring bad luck

Example: I must have put a jinx on her.

jive /ˈdʒaɪv/

a lively jerky dance that was popular in the 1940s and 1950s

Example: Her Jive kicks and flicks are superb.

job /dʒˈɔːb/

a person's occupation or paid employment

Example: Teaching is actually a very rewarding job.

jockey /ˈdʒɔki/

a person who rides horses in races as a profession

Example: He is a very confident jockey.

joiner /ˈdʒɔɪnɚ/

a person whose job is making finished woodwork

Example: You're a carpenter and joiner by trade.

joinery /ˈdʒɔɪnɚi/

the skill or work of a joiner

Example: The city has therefore chosen joinery and cabinetmaking as this sample.

joist /ˈdʒɔɪst/

a beam made of timber, steel, or concrete, used as a support in the construction of floors and roofs

Example: Wooden ceiling beams will be turned into benches, and floor joists will become stairs.

joke /ˈdʒok/

something that is said or done to amuse people

Example: Did I tell you the joke about the chicken crossing the road?

jolt /ˈdʒoʊlt/

a severe shock

Example: I woke up with a jolt as I thought I heard my bedroom door being pushed open.

journal /ˈdʒɝnəl/

a newspaper or magazine

Example: She kept a travel journal during her trip to South America.

journalese /ˌdʒɝnəˈliz/

a superficial style of writing regarded as typical of newspapers and magazines

Example: Journalese was getting out of hand again.

journalism /ˈdʒɝnəˌlɪzəm/

the profession of collecting, writing, and publishing news through newspapers and magazines or by radio and television

Example: She sees her experience in journalism as one of the keys to her success.

journalist /ˈdʒɝnələst/

a person who writes or edits news items for a newspaper or magazine or for radio or television

Example: This is a real problem for journalists now.

journey /ˈdʒɝni/

the process of traveling from one place to another

Example: The journey takes five and a half hours.

jowl /ˈdʒaʊl/

the fatty flesh hanging from the lower jaw

Example: His fat jowls quivered unhappily around his cigar while he counted out the bills.

joy /dʒˈɔɪ/

deep happiness and contentment

Example: They were filled with joy when their first child was born.

jubilation /ˌdʒubəˈleɪʃən/

a feeling of great joy and celebration

Example: You have heard from families, witnessed the jubilation.

judge /dʒˈʌdʒ/

a public official with the authority to hear cases and pass sentences in a court of law

Example: There was a disagreement between the high court judge and the appeal court judges.

judgment /dʒˈʌdʒmənt/

a decision formed after careful consideration

Example: Shareholders should back the company's judgement and take up their rights.

judiciary /dʒuˈdɪʃiˌɛri/

the branch of the central authority in a country that administers justice

Example: We need a judiciary that protects the rights of all our citizens

jug /ˈdʒʌg/

a container with a handle and a small spout, used for holding and pouring liquids

Example: She filled the jug up with cream.

jugular /ˈdʒugjəlɚ/

a large vein in the neck that carries blood to the heart from the head

Example: Her jugular vein was cut, and she sadly passed away, bleeding to death.

juice /ˈdʒus/

a drink made from the liquid part of a fruit or vegetable

Example: Taste and adjust the seasoning with salt, pepper, and lemon juice.

jukebox /ˈdʒukˌbɔks/

an automatic coin-operated record player

Example: The jukebox musical is a godsend to pop stars.

jumble /ˈdʒəmbəl/

a disordered mass or state

Example: The set is an uninspiring jumble.

junction /ˈdʒəŋkʃən/

a place where roads or railway lines meet, link, or cross each other

Example: They were at what appeared a junction of several tracks.

juncture /ˈdʒəŋktʃɚ/

a point in time, especially a critical one

Example: Negotiations are at a critical juncture.

jungle /ˈdʒəŋgəl/

a forest area in a hot country with luxuriant vegetation

Example: They set off with him at dawn on a hike through a dense jungle.

junk /ˈdʒʌŋk/

old or unwanted objects

Example: I cleared all the junk out of the garage.

junket /ˈdʒəŋkɪt/
an excursion made by a public official and paid for out of public funds
Example: Publishers will continue the junkets because they work.

jurisdiction /ˌdʒʊrəsˈdɪkʃən/
to right or power to administer justice and to apply laws
Example: A law passed in 2006 sought to strip the federal courts of jurisdiction to consider the detainees' plight.

jurisprudence /ˌdʒʊrəsˈpɹudəns/
the science or philosophy of law
Example: He might have altered the course of capital penalty jurisprudence.

jurist /ˈdʒʊrəst/
a person who is an expert on law
Example: He is an acclaimed jurist.

juror /ˈdʒʊrɚ/
a member of a jury
Example: The Juror was invited to join the meeting.

jury /ˈdʒʊri/
a group of, usually, twelve people, sworn to deliver a true verdict according to the evidence upon a case presented in a court of law
Example: An earlier jury was unable to reach a verdict.

justice /ˈd͡ʒʌstɪs/
the quality of being just
Example: We need to see these men brought to justice.

Kk

kaleidoscope /kəˈlaɪdəˌskoʊp/

a tube-shaped toy lined with angled mirrors and containing loose pieces of coloured paper that form intricate patterns when viewed through a hole in the end

Example: *I loved kaleidoscope when I was a kid.*

any complicated or rapidly changing set of colours, circumstances, etc.

Example: *At sunset, the sky became a kaleidoscope of colours.*

kangaroo /ˌkæŋgɚˈu/

a large Australian marsupial with powerful hind legs used for leaping

Example: *The kangaroo has a fast turn of speed.*

kaolin /ˈkaʊlɪn/

a fine white clay used in making porcelain and in some medicines

Example: *I prescribed a kaolin antacid mixture to be given in the morning and evening.*

karaoke /ˌkɛriˈoʊki/

a form of entertainment in which members of the public sing well-known songs over a prerecorded backing tape

Example: *They can relax by singing at a karaoke bar.*

karate /kɚˈɑti/

a Japanese system of unarmed combat, in which punches, chops, and kicks are made with the hands, feet, elbows, and legs

Example: *She enrolled in karate to help restore her confidence after the mugging.*

kayak /ˈkaɪæk/

an Inuit canoe-like boat consisting of a frame covered with animal skins

Example: *Everybody loved the ride in the kayak.*

kebab /kəˈbɑb/

a dish consisting of small pieces of meat and vegetables, usually threaded onto skewers and grilled

Example: Fried rice will be perfect with the Chicken Kebab.

keel /ˈkiɫ/

one of the main lengthways steel or timber pieces along the base of a ship, to which the frames are fastened

Example: The yacht's keel is bolted to the hull.

keg /ˈkɛg/

a small barrel in which beer is transported and stored

Example: The bartender tapped a new keg of beer.

kelp /ˈkɛlp/

a large brown seaweed rich in iodine and potash

Example: They cultivated kelp off the seashore of their village.

kennel /ˈkɛnəl/

a hut-like shelter for a dog

Example: They keep their dog in an outdoor kennel.

keratin /ˈkɛrətən/

a fibrous protein found in the hair and nails.

Example: The sulfurous smell of Burning keratin is distinctive.

kerchief /ˈkɝtʃəf/

a piece of cloth worn over the head or round the neck

Example: Jozia blew her red nose into her kerchief.

ketch /ˈkɛtʃ/

a two-masted sailing ship

Example: A ketch is a common rig for cruising sailboats.

ketchup /ˈkɛtʃəp/

a thick cold sauce, usually made from tomatoes

Example: There's a spot of ketchup on the tablecloth.

kettle /ˈkɛtəl/

a metal container with a handle and spout, for boiling water

Example: Pour a kettle of boiling water over the onions.

key /kˈiː/

a specially shaped metal instrument, for moving the bolt of a lock so as to lock or unlock a door, suitcase, etc.

Example: He turned the key in the lock.

any of a set of levers pressed to operate a typewriter, computer, or musical keyboard instrument

Example: Every key on the piano produces a different sound.

something that is crucial in providing an explanation or interpretation

Example: He has the key to the map.

keynote /ˈkiˌnoʊt/

a central or dominant idea in a speech or literary work

Example: World peace was the keynote of his speech.

keypad /ˈkiˌpæd/

a small panel with a set of buttons for operating a Teletext system, electronic calculator, etc.

Example: Punch your credit card number into the keypad.

keystone /ˈkiˌstoʊn/

the most important part of a process, organization, etc.

Example: Social justice is the keystone of their political program.

keyword /ˈkiˌwɜ-d/

a word or phrase that a computer will search for in order to locate the information or file that the computer user has requested

Example: You can find the site by entering the keyword 'Quark'.

kidney /ˈkɪdni/

either of two bean-shaped organs at the back of the abdominal cavity that filter waste products from the blood, which are excreted as urine

Example: He was being treated for kidney failure.

kiln /ˈkɪln/

a large oven for burning, drying, or processing pottery, bricks, etc.

Example: The bricks are left in the kiln to bake.

kilobyte /ˈkɪloʊˌbaɪt/

1024 bytes

Example: You need a machine with 64 kilobytes of memory to run the program.

kilogram /ˈkɪləˌgræm/

one thousand grams

Example: Apples are sold by the kilogram.

kilometer /ˌkɪˈlɔˌmətɚ/

a unit of length equal to one thousand meters

Example: He can swim two kilometers.

kin /ˈkɪn/

a person's relatives collectively

Example: We have notified the next of kin of the boy's tragic death.

kind /kˈaɪnd/

a class or group having characteristics in common

Example: The flowers are all the same kind.

kindergarten /ˈkɪndɚˌgɑrtən/

a class or school for children under six years old

Example: There is a kindergarten behind my house.

kindness /kˈaɪndnəs/

the quality of being kind

Example: Her kindness of heart endeared her to everyone.

kinetics /kəˈnɛtɪks/

the branch of mechanics concerned with the study of bodies in motion

Example: He understood the kinetics of the robot through hard work.

king /kˈɪŋ/

a male ruler of a country who has inherited the throne from his parents

Example: The King was clothed in a purple gown.

kingdom /ˈkɪŋdəm/

a territory or state ruled by a king or queen

Example: He ruled the ancient kingdom of Kafka.

any of the three groups into which natural objects may be divided: the animal, plant, and mineral kingdoms

Example: They are five animal kingdoms.

kingfisher /ˈkɪŋˌfɪʃɚ/

a fish-eating bird with a greenish-blue and orange plumage

Example: The Australian kingfisher has a loud cackling cry.

kingpin /ˈkɪŋˌpɪn/

the most important person in an organization

Example: He's the kingpin of the whole criminal enterprise.

kinship /ˈkɪnˌʃɪp/

blood relationship

Example: The sense of kinship between the two men is surprising.

kinsman /ˈkɪnzˌmæn/

a relation by blood or marriage

Example: The trip was cut short by the death of a close kinsman.

kismet /ˈkɪzmɪt/

fate or destiny

Example: Our change in direction was kismet.

kiss /kˈɪs/

a caress with the lips

Example: She stood on tiptoe to kiss him.

kit /ˈkɪt/

a set of tools or supplies use together or for a common purpose

Example: There should be a needle and thread in the sewing kit.

kitchen /ˈkɪtʃən/

a room equipped for preparing and cooking food

Example: Delicious smells were emanating from the kitchen.

kitchenette /ˌkɪtʃəˈnɛt/

a small kitchen or part of a room equipped for use as a kitchen

Example: She is living with her daughter in one room with a kitchenette.

kite /ˈkaɪt/

a light frame covered with a thin material flown in the wind at the end of a length of string

Example: There is not enough wind to fly a kite.

kitsch /ˈkɪtʃ/

tawdry or sentimental art or literature

Example: That new lamp they have bought is pure kitsch.

kitten /ˈkɪtən/

a young cat

Example: Our cat gave birth to five kittens.

kitty /ˈkɪti/

the pool in certain gambling games

Example: You have not put any money in the kitty for three weeks.

kiwi /ˈkiwi/

a flightless bird of New Zealand with a long beak, stout legs, and no tail

Example: The kiwi eats worms, other invertebrates, and berries.

an edible fruit with a fuzzy brown skin and green flesh

Example: Decorate the fruit salad with a slice of starfruit and kiwi.

knack /ˈnæk/

a skillful way of doing something

Example: She has a knack of making friends.

knapsack /ˈnæpˌsæk/

a canvas or leather bag carried strapped on the back or shoulder

Example: He had a knapsack over his shoulder.

knee /ˈni/

the joint of the leg between the thigh and the lower leg

Example: I felt a twinge in my knee.

knell /ˈnɛl/

something that indicates death or destruction

Example: It sounded the knell of all her hopes.

knickers /ˈnɪkɜ-z/

a woman's or girl's undergarment covering the lower trunk and having separate legs or leg-holes

Example: Tight bras and knickers can cause unsightly bulges under close-fitting clothes.

knife /nˈaɪf/

a cutting instrument or weapon consisting of a sharp-edged blade of metal fitted into a handle

Example: Trim rough edges with a sharp knife.

knight /ˈnaɪt/

a man who has been given a knighthood in recognition of his achievements

Example: The knight spurred on to the castle.

knighthood /ˈnaɪtˌhʊd/

an honorary title given to a man by the British sovereign in recognition of his achievements

Example: He was honoured with a knighthood.

knob /ˈnɔb/

a rounded handle of a door or drawer

Example: She turned the knob of the door carefully.

a small amount of butter or margarine

Example: Put a knob of butter in the frying pan.

knoll /ˈnoʊɫ/

a small rounded hill

Example: He crawled up a small knoll and surveyed the prospect.

knot /ˈnɔt/

a fastening formed by looping and tying pieces of rope, cord, or string

Example: Tie the two ropes together with a secure knot.

a small cluster or huddled group

Example: Little knots of people had gathered at the entrance.

a bond

Example: They tied the knot.

a hard mass of wood where a branch joins the trunk of a tree

Example: The branch was hanging from the knot.

a feeling of tightness, caused by tension or nervousness

Example: Her nimble fingers undid the knot in seconds.

a unit of speed used by ships and aircraft, equal to one nautical mile per hour

Example: The vessel's maximum cruising speed is 35 knots.

knowledge /nˈɔːlɪdʒ/

the facts or experiences known by a person or group of people

Example: Imagination will span the gap in our knowledge.

knuckle /ˈnəkəl/

a joint of a finger

Example: Our fingers bend at the knuckle.

krypton /ˈkrɪptɑn/

an inert gaseous element occurring in trace amounts in air and used in fluorescent lights and lasers

Example: The Krypton gas-peril of the new reprocessing plant in Cumbria has been exposed by the Mirror.

kung fu /ˈkəŋ ˈfu/

a Chinese martial art combining techniques of karate and judo

Example: Kung fu and karate are martial arts.

Ll

lab /lˈɑb/

a laboratory

Example: The professor took the students to the chemistry lab.

label /ˈleɪbəl/

a piece of card or other material attached to an object to show its contents, ownership, use, or destination

Example: The washing instructions are on the label.

laboratory /ˈlæbrəˌtɔri/

a building or room equipped for conducting scientific research or for teaching practical science

Example: They work in a laboratory studying growth patterns.

labour /ˈleɪbɚ/

productive work, especially physical work done for wages

Example: People look forward to enjoying the fruits of their labour after hard work.

the final stage of pregnancy, leading to childbirth

Example: She went into labour early.

labourer /ˈleɪbɚ/

a person engaged in physical work

Example: Her husband had been a farm labourer.

ladder /lˈædɚ/

a portable frame consisting of two long parallel supports connected by steps, for climbing up or down

Example: Dad was up the ladder, repairing the roof.

any system thought of as having a series of ascending stages

Example: He who would climb the ladder must begin at the bottom.

lady /lˈeɪdi/

a woman regarded as having the characteristics of a good family, such as dignified manners

Example: She was with an attractive young lady.

lake /lˈeɪk/

an expanse of water entirely surrounded by land

Example: The boys swam across the lake.

a bright pigment produced by combining organic colouring matter with an inorganic compound

Example: The lake was polluted because of the miners.

landlady /lˈændleɪdi/

a woman who owns and leases property

Example: The landlady came around once a month to collect the rent.

landlord /lˈændlɔːrd/

a man who owns and leases property

Example: The landlord was willing to accept us as tenants.

language /lˈaŋgwɪdʒ/

a system of spoken sounds or conventional symbols for communicating thought

Example: *Every language has its own idioms.*

laughter /l'æftɚ/

the action or noise of laughing

Example: *His hysterical laughter surprised everybody.*

law /l'ɔː/

a rule or set of rules regulating what may or may not be done by members of a society or community

Example: *The new law comes into force next month.*

leader /l'iːdɚ/

a person who rules, guides, or inspires others

Example: *She is born to be a leader.*

the best or the most successful of its kind

Example: *Jake was appraised of being the most dedicated leader of all his peers.*

leadership /l'iːdɚʃˌɪp/

the action of leading a group of people or an organization

Example: *John was named the leadership of the football team.*

leaf /l'iːf/

one of the flat usually green blades attached to the stem of a plant

Example: *The ground was thick with dead leaves.*

length /l'ɛŋθ/

the extent of measurement of something from end to end

Example: *He measured the length and width of the table.*

the amount of trouble taken in doing something

Example: *He went to great length to prepare a delicious meal for his mom.*

level /l'ɛvəl/

a horizontal line or plane

Example: They hung the pictures at eye level.

a device for determining whether a surface is horizontal

Example: The carpenter used the level to measure the windows.

liberty /lˈɪbɚɾi/

the freedom to choose, think, and act for oneself

Example: The city won its liberty in the sixteenth century.

library /lˈaɪbrɛri/

a room or building where books and other literary materials are kept

Example: They will transfer those books into the new library.

lice /lˈaɪs/

wingless blood-sucking insects that feed off man and some animals

Example: Her hair was crawling with lice.

life /lˈaɪf/

the state or quality that identifies living beings, characterized chiefly by growth, reproduction, and response to stimuli

Example: In spring the countryside bursts into life.

light /lˈaɪt/

the natural medium, electromagnetic radiation, that makes sight possible; anything that illuminates

Example: The light beams through the wall on the house.

line /lˈaɪn/

a narrow continuous mark, such as one made by a pencil

Example: John drew a line to join all the crosses.

a boundary

Example: Tim draws the line.

linguistics /lɪŋɡwˈɪstɪks/

the scientific study of language

Example: His linguistic ability served him well in his chosen profession.

link /lˈɪŋk/

a connecting part or episode

Example: The study demonstrates the link between poverty and malnutrition.

any of the separate rings that form a chain

Example: The jeweler made various amounts of link to create Sarah's necklace.

an emotional or logical relationship between people or things

Example: The two of them shared a great link.

lion /lˈaɪən/

a large animal of the cat family found in Africa and India, with a tawny yellow coat, and a shaggy mane

Example: The lion was lying in his den.

lioness /lˈaɪənɛs/

a female lion

Example: The lioness gave birth to a beautiful cub.

list /lˈɪst/

an item-by-item record of names or things, usually written one below the other

Example: Mummy prepared a list of items that she needed from the shop.

literature /lˈɪtɚrɪtʃɚ/

written material such as poetry, novels, or essays

Example: The literature he prepared has amazing content.

loaf /lˈoʊf/

a shaped or molded mass of food, such as cooked meat and bread

Example: The loaf of bread is filled with mold.

location /lookˈeɪʃən/

a site or position

Example: They placed the location into Google maps for directions.

loneliness /lˈoʊnlinəs/

sadness because one has no friends or company

Example: Grandma has felt keen loneliness since her husband passed away.

the quality of being unfrequented and remote

Example: The street is said to be filled with loneliness.

loss /lˈɔs/

the act or an instance of losing

Example: The party suffered a great loss.

louse /lˈaʊs/

a wingless blood-sucking insects that feed off man and some animals

Example: The dog's owner ensured that his pet had not a singlelouse.

love /lˈʌv/

an intense emotion of affection towards a person or thing

Example: They showed great love towards each other.

luck /lˈʌk/

events that are subject to chance, fortune, good or bad

Example: He tried his luck at the game and won lots of money.

luxury /lˈʌkʃɚri/

indulgence in rich and sumptuous living

Example: She had a life filled with luxury.

Mm

machine /məʃˈiːn/

an assembly of components arranged so as to perform a particular task and usually powered by electricity

Example: Uncle Roy placed all his clothes in the washing machine.

madam /mɑdəm/

a polite term of address for a woman

Example: It is better to start the letter with dear madam.

a woman who runs a brothel

Example: The madam collects all the money before she allows anybody to enter.

magazine /ˌmagəzˈiːn/

a periodic paperback publication containing written pieces and illustrations

Example: This neighbour has the magazine with all the latest hits.

a metal case holding several cartridges used in some firearms

Example: The soldier has a magazine hiding under his pants.

a rack for automatically feeding slides through a projector

Example: One by one the girls flip the magazine during their presentation.

a place for storing weapons, explosives, or military equipment

Example: Before the battle they all lined up at the magazine depot to collect their supplies.

maintenance /mˈeɪntənəns/

the act of maintaining or the state of being maintained

Example: The building lacked maintenance, hence it is reason for falling apart.

financial provision ordered to be made by way of periodical payments or a lump sum, usually for a separated or divorced spouse

Example: The court ordered him to pay a strict maintenance fee every month.

mall /mˈɔːl/

a large enclosed shopping centre

Example: Uncle Ted carried his children to the mall for an ice-cream date.

man /mˈan/

an adult male human being

Example: He's a man of many talents.

management /mˈanɪdʒmənt/

the people responsible for running an organization or business

Example: Each apartment had strict management.

manager /mˈanɪdʒɚ/

a person who manages an organization or business

Example: Sarah was awarded with the position of a manager at the store.

manufacturer /mˌanjuːfˈæktʃərɚ/

a person or company that makes goods for sale

Example: The manufacturer ensures that each item is screened before shipping.

map /mˈap/

a diagrammatic representation of the earth's surface or part of it, showing the geographical distributions or positions of features such as roads, towns, etc.

Example: The map helped us to find our way to the park.

market /mˈaːrkɪt/

a place where people meet to buy and sell goods and services

Example: Each Saturday many people visit the market for their weekly supply of vegetables.

marketing /mˈaːrkɪrɪŋ/

the part of a business which controls the way that goods or services are sold

Example: The marketing committee continues to add taxes to small items.

marriage /mˈarɪdʒ/

the state or relationship of being husband and wife

Example: Marriage has many ups and downs.

masculinity /ˌmæskjəˈlɪnəti/

qualities or attributes regarded as characteristic of men or boys

Example: He stood up for his girlfriend by demonstrating his masculinity.

master /mˈæstɚ/

the man who has authority over others, such as the head of a household, the employer of servants, etc.

Example: My father is the master of the house.

a person with exceptional skill at a certain thing

Example: He was the master of throwing knives.

a person who has complete control of a situation

Example: Jake continues to master his temper.

an original copy or tape from which duplicates are made

Example: He sold all the master movies.

material /mətˈɪriəl/

the substance of which a thing is made

Example: Kayla's dress was sewn with different materials.

math /mˈaθ/

a group of related sciences, including algebra, geometry, and calculus, which use a specialized notation to study number, quantity, shape, and space

Example: Augustus is best at teaching math.

matrix /mˈeɪtrɪks/

the context or framework in which something is formed or develops

Example: A basic grounding in matrix is essential for the economics course.

the rock in which fossils or pebbles are embedded

Example: The stones consist of pieces of matrix.

matter /mˈætɚ/

substance that occupies space and has mass, as distinguished from substance that is mental or spiritual

Example: The matter changed from a solid to a liquid form when it was placed in the sun to melt.

an event, situation, or subject

Example: She may need your help with a business matter.

maturity /mətʃˈʊrɪti/

the state, fact, or period of being fully developed physically or mentally

Example: She has shown great maturity in her behavior this term.

meal /mˈiːl/

the food served and eaten

Example: The family was always noisy during their meals.

the edible part of a grain or bean pulse ground to a coarse powder

Example: The farmer grinds the rice to make a meal for his fowls.

meaning /mˈiːnɪŋ/

the sense or significance of a word, sentence, or symbol

Example: Each student gave different meaning of the sign they saw on the tour.

means /mˈiːnz/

the medium, method, or instrument used to obtain a result or achieve an end

Example: They are different ways and means of making money.

measurement /mˈɛʒɚmənt/

a system or unit used for measuring

Example: The test is based on the measurement of blood levels.

meat /mˈiːt/

the flesh of animal used as food

Example: We should only eat the meat from the chicken.

the essence or gist

Example: Let us get right to the meat of the matter and address the problem.

media /mˈiːdiːə/

the main means of mass communication

Example: Most families communicate through the media.

medicine /mˈɛdəsən/

any substance used in treating or alleviating the symptoms of disease

Example: Mr. Steve was shown improvement in his health after taking his medicine.

medium /mˈiːdiəm/

a middle state, degree, or condition

Example: He was a man of medium height.

a means for communicating information or news to the public

Example: Radio is an important communication medium in many countries.

member /mˈɛmbɚ/

a person who belongs to a group or organization such as a club or political party

Example: He was selected to be a member of the group.

membership /mˈɛmbɚˌʃɪp/

the members of an organization collectively

Example: The company has a large membership.

memory /mˈɛmɚri/

the ability of the mind to store and recall past sensations, thoughts, and knowledge

Example: He suffered memory loss for weeks after the accident.

men /mˈɛn/

two or more adult male human beings

Example: The group of men were sitting together after a long day of work.

menu /mˈɛnjuː/

a list of dishes served at a meal or that can be ordered in a restaurant

Example: The restaurant has an extensive menu and daily specials.

message /mˈɛsɪdʒ/

a communication from one person or group to another

Example: I left a message on your answering machine.

an implicit meaning or moral, as in a work of art

Example: His drawing sent a very emotional message.

metal /mˈɛtəl/

a chemical element, such as iron or copper, that reflects light and can be shaped, forms positive ions, and is a good conductor of heat and electricity

Example: The metal has corroded over time because of rust.

method /mˈɛθəd/

a way of doing something, especially a systematic or regular one

Example: Their method of teaching math is very interesting.

mice /mˈaɪs/

two or more small long-tailed rodents similar to but smaller than a rat

Example: Mr.Lee's kitchen is filled with mice.

midnight /mˈɪdnaɪt/

the middle of the night

Example: The team is set to ride at midnight.

milkman /mˈɪlkmən/

a man who delivers milk to people's houses

Example: Every morning the milkman delivers the milk.

mind /mˈaɪnd/

the part of a person responsible for thoughts, feelings, and intention

Example: His mind is as sharp as ever.

mistress /mˈɪstrəs/

a woman who has a continuing sexual relationship with a man who is usually married to someone else

Example: His wife suspected that the woman she had seen with him was his mistress.

mixture /mˈɪkstʃɚ/

something produced by blending or combining different things

Example: Concrete is a mixture of sand and cement.

mob /mˈɔːb/

a riotous or disorderly crowd of people

Example: They were all a part of the violent mob.

mode /mˈoʊd/

a manner or way of doing, acting, or existing

Example: His mode of doing business is offensive to me.

model /mˈɑːdəl/

a three-dimensional representation, usually on a smaller scale, of a device or structure

Example: The organization created an airplane model.

an example or pattern that people might want to follow

Example: The officer continues to be a role model for the younger children.

a person who poses for a sculptor, painter, or photographer

Example: She is the model for the show.

a theoretical description of the way a system or process works

Example: The model consists of a detailed description of how each equipment in the building functions.

moment /mˈoʊmənt/

a short period of time

Example: It will only take me a moment to get dressed.

a specific instant or point in time

Example: This is the only moment you must shine.

money /mˈʌni/

a means of payment and measure of value

Example: He dropped the money he owed the farmer.

the official currency, in the form of banknotes or coins, issued by a government

Example: Where can I change my money into dollars?

month /mˈʌnθ/

one of the twelve divisions of the calendar year

Example: The rally is set to start in the second month of next year.

mood /mˈuːd/

a temporary state of mind or temper

Example: He was in no mood for being polite to visitors.

a prevailing atmosphere or feeling

Example: The flower set in the hall set the mood.

moonlight /mˈuːnlaɪt/

light from the sun received on earth after reflection by the moon

Example: The moonlight was our guide through the night.

moose /mˈuːs/

a large North American deer with large flattened antlers

Example: The bull moose was on the loose.

morning /mˈɔːrnɪŋ/

the first part of the day, ending at noon

Example: We will leave in the morning.

mosquito /məskˈiːtoʊ/

a two-winged insect, the females of which pierce the skin of humans and animals to suck their blood

Example: Mosquito season is approaching, so prepare the nets.

mouse /mˈaʊs/

a small long-tailed rodent similar to but smaller than a rat

Example: Try as he might, he could not trap the mouse.

movie /mˈuːvi/

a cinema film

Example: Let us go to the theatre to watch a movie.

mud /mˈʌd/

soft wet earth, as found on the ground after rain or at the bottom of ponds

Example: The dog loves rolling in the mud.

music /mjˈuːzɪk/

an art form consisting of sequences of sounds organized melodically, harmonically, and rhythmically

Example: The sound of martial music is always inspiring.

Nn

nail /ˈneɪl/

a piece of metal with a point at one end and a head on the other

Example: He hammered the nail into the wood.

the hard covering of the upper tips of the fingers and toes

Example: You should stop biting your nails.

name /nˈeɪm/

a word or term by which a person or thing is known

Example: The company reopened under a new name.

a reputation, especially a good one

Example: He created a good name for himself.

nameplate /ˈneɪmˌpleɪt/

a small sign on or next to a door giving the occupant's name and, sometimes, profession

Example: This nameplate has been over the company gate for thirty years.

namesake /ˈneɪmˌseɪk/

a person or thing with the same name as another

Example: She's my namesake but we are not related.

nanny /ˈnɑni/

a woman whose job is looking after young children

Example: They have a male nanny for their kids.

nap /ˈnɑp/

a short sleep

Example: I want to take a nap.

naphtha /ˈnæfθə/

a liquid mixture distilled from coal tar or petroleum, used as a solvent and in petrol

Example: He produced the desired results by joining two sheets of fabric with dissolved India rubber soaked in naphtha.

naphthalene /ˈnæfθəˌlin/

a white crystalline substance distilled from coal tar or petroleum, used in mothballs, dyes, and explosives

Example: He uses naphthalene balls for his clothes.

napkin /ˈnapkɪn/

a piece of cloth or paper for wiping the mouth or protecting the clothes while eating

Example: He tucked his napkin under his chin.

narcissism /ˈnɑrsɪˌsɪzəm/

an exceptional interest in or admiration for oneself

Example: The performance was dominated by the preening narcissism of the group's lead singer.

narcotic /nɑrˈkɔtɪk/

a drug, such as opium or morphine, that produces numbness and drowsiness, used medicinally but addictive

Example: He has been arrested for trading in narcotics.

narration /nɛˈreɪʃən/

a narrated account or story

Example: The richness of his novel comes from his narration of it.

narrative /ˈnɑrətɪv/

the part of a literary work that relates events

Example: People have always tried to create narratives through stories and painting.

narrator /ˈnɑrətɚ/

the fictional character or authorial voice relating events in a story or novel

Example: The narrator in the novel is not a dependable witness.

nation /ˈneɪʃən/

a large body of people of one or more cultures or races, organized into a single state

Example: He represented the nation on ceremonial occasions.

nationalism /ˈnæʃənəˌlɪzəm/

a policy of national independence

Example: The novel is really a dissection of nationalism.

nationality /ˌnæʃəˈnæləti/

the fact of being a citizen of a particular nation

Example: She lives in America, but her nationality is Guyanese.

nativity /nəˈtɪvəti/

birth or origin

Example: They visited the place of Jesus' nativity.

naturalism /ˈnætʃɚəˌlɪzəm/

a movement in art and literature advocating detailed realism

Example: The Darwinian worldview is the view of evolutionary naturalism.

naturalist /ˈnætʃɚələst/

a student of natural history

Example: Sam was also a keen and talented naturalist.

nature /ˈneɪtʃɚ/

the whole system of the existence, forces, and events of the physical world that are not controlled by human beings

Example: It is the nature of every man to err, but only the fool perseveres in the error.

nausea /ˈnɔziə/

the feeling of being about to vomit

Example: He was overcome with nausea after eating some bad food.

nave /ˈneɪv/

the long central part of a church

Example: The elders were gathered in the nave.

the hub of a wheel

Example: The riders depended on the hub of the wheel for balance.

navel /ˈneɪvəl/

the slight hollow in the center of the abdomen, where the umbilical cord was attached

Example: *She had an emerald in her navel.*

navy /ˈneɪvi/

the branch of a country's armed services comprising warships with their crew, and all their supporting services

Example: *Two of the soldiers bunked up together in the Navy.*

nebulizer /ˈnɛbjəˌlaɪzɚ/

a device which turns a drug from a liquid into a fine spray which can be inhaled

Example: *The patient needs a nebulizer at his bedside immediately.*

necessity /nəˈsɛsəti/

a set of circumstances that inevitably requires a certain result

Example: *He emphasized the necessity of taking strong measures.*

something needed

Example: *These things are our necessity.*

neck /ˈnɛk/

the part of the body connecting the head with the rest of the body

Example: *He tied a scarf around his neck.*

necklace /ˈnɛkləs/

a decorative piece of jewellery worn round the neck

Example: *A heavy gold necklace hung around her neck.*

nectar /ˈnɛktɚ/

sugary fluid produced by flowers and collected by bees

Example: *Bees turn nectar into honey.*

need /nˈiːd/

the condition of lacking something

Example: We need new pair of shoes.

necessity

Example: We need oxygen to survive.

needle /ˈnidəl/

a pointed slender piece of metal with a hole in it through which thread is passed for sewing

Example: She sewed it on with needle and thread.

negation /nəˈgeɪʃən/

the opposite or absence of something

Example: Much of what passes for Christianity is a negation of Christ's teachings.

negligence /ˈnɛglədʒəns/

neglect or careless

Example: He threatened to sue the company for negligence.

negotiation /nɪgˌoʊʃɪˈeɪʃən/

discussion aimed at reaching an agreement

Example: The proposal is now under negotiation.

neighbour /ˈneɪbɚ/

a person who lives near or next to another

Example: She's been a very good neighbour to me.

neighbourhood /ˈneɪbɚˌhʊd/

a district where people live

Example: My neighbourhood has really been built up.

nemesis /ˈnɛməsɪs/

a means of retribution or vengeance

Example: She had finally met her nemesis.

neon /ˈniɔɑn/

a colourless odourless rare gas, used in illuminated signs and lights

Example: Colourful neon lights were hung here and there during National Day.

neophyte /ˈniəˌfaɪt/

a person newly converted to a religious faith

Example: He is a neophyte at politics.

nephew /ˈnɛfju/

a son of one's sister or brother

Example: He asked his nephew to execute his will.

nerve /ˈnɝv/

a cordlike bundle of fibres that conducts impulses between the brain and other parts of the body

Example: The nerve runs from the eye to the brain.

nestling /ˈnɛslɪŋ/

a young bird not yet able to fly

Example: She fluttered around me like a mother bird at her nestlings.

network /nˈɛtwɜːk/

an interconnecting group or system

Example: All our computers are plugged into the main network.

neurology /nʊˈrɔlədʒi/

the scientific study of the nervous system

Example: He trained in neurology at the National Hospital for Nervous Diseases.

neurosis /nʊˈroʊsəs/

a mental disorder producing hysteria, anxiety, depression, or obsessive behavior

Example: He may have neurosis or psychosis later in life.

neurosurgery /ˌnʊroʊˈsɜ-dʒɚ-i/

the branch of surgery concerned with the nervous system

Example: I would get the neurosurgery resident down here to do a physical examination.

neutron /ˈnuˌtrɔn/

a neutral elementary particle of about the same mass as a proton

Example: The proton has positive electrical charge; the neutron has none.

newcomer /ˈnuˌkəmɚ/

a recent arrival or participant

Example: The newcomer is not used to the heavy traffic in big cities.

news /nˈuːz/

information about important or interesting new happening

Example: Headlines blazed the most exciting news.

newscast /ˈnuzˌkæst/

a radio or television broadcast of the news

Example: They watched as a television newscast reported that the candidate is still alive

newspaper /nˈuːzpeɪpɚ/

a weekly or daily publication containing news, features, and advertisements

Example: The newspaper reported on Friday that the boy had been found.

newsroom /ˈnuzˌrum/

a room in a newspaper office or radio or television station where news is received and prepared for publication or broadcasting

Example: The message will be transmitted directly to the newsroom.

newton /ˈnutən/

the SI unit of force that gives an acceleration of 1 metre per second per second to a mass of 1 kilogram

Example: *The unit of force is the newton where one newton is one kilogram meter per second squared.*

niacin /ˈnaɪəsən/

a vitamin of the B complex that occurs in milk, liver, and yeast

Example: *A lack of niacin causes pellagra, dermatitis, diarrhea, dementia embolism.*

nicety /ˈnaɪsɪti/

a refinement or delicacy

Example: *The restaurant offered a small nicety at the end of our meal.*

nickel /ˈnɪkəl/

a silvery-white metallic element that is often used in alloys

Example: *About 60 percent of nickel production is used to make stainless steel.*

niece /nˈiːs/

a daughter of one's sister or brother

Example: *The behaviour of my niece is beginning to concern me.*

niggard /ˈnɪgɚd/

a stingy person

Example: *He is a niggard.*

night /nˈaɪt/

the period of darkness that occurs each 24 hours, between sunset and sunrise

Example: *Last night they stayed at home and watched television.*

nightclub /ˈnaɪtˌkləb/

a place of entertainment open until late at night, offering drinks and dancing

Example: *She's performing at a nightclub in Paris.*

nightfall /ˈnaɪtˌfɔl/

the approach of darkness

Example: We hope to be back by nightfall.

nightingale /ˈnaɪtɪŋgeɪl/

a small bird with a musical song, usually heard at night

Example: You can hear a nightingale whistle at night.

nightlife /ˈnaɪtˌlaɪf/

the entertainment and social activities available at night in a town or city

Example: The main attraction of the place is the nightlife.

nightmare /ˈnaɪtˌmɛr/

a terrifying or deeply distressing dream or experience

Example: I had a nightmare about being drowned in a lake.

nihilism /ˈnaɪəˌlɪzəm/

a total rejection of all established authority and institutions

Example: Nihilism rejects any objective basis for society and its morality.

nipple /ˈnɪpəl/

the small projection in the centre of each breast, which in females contains the outlet of the milk ducts

Example: Nipple inversion is quite common in normal breasts.

nit /ˈnɪt/

the egg or larvae of a louse

Example: They were many nits hiding in the drawer.

nobility /noʊˈbɪləti/

the quality of being noble and dignified

Example: Her nobility of character made her much admired.

nock /ˈnɑk/

a notch on an arrow that fits on the bowstring

Example: The nock is relatively small, typical of that attached to the lower limb of the bow.

noise /ˈnɔɪz/

a sound, usually loud and disturbing

Example: There was too much noise in the room, and he needed peace.

nomad /ˈnoʊˌmæd/

a member of a tribe who moves from place to place to find pasture and food

Example: What did this desert nomad make of that?

nominee /ˌnɑməˈni/

a person who is nominated to an office or as a candidate

Example: I was delighted to be a nominee and to receive such a prestigious award.

noncombatant /ˌnɑnkəmˈbætənt/

a member of the armed forces whose duties do not include fighting, such as a chaplain or surgeon

Example: The General does not like noncombatant personnel near a scene of action.

nonconformist /ˌnɑnkənˈfɔrmɪst/

a person who does not conform to generally accepted patterns of behavior or thought

Example: His father was a nonconformist minister.

nonentity /nʌnɛntəti/

an insignificant person or thing

Example: How could such a nonentity become chairman of the company?

nonevent /ˈnʌnɪˈvɛnt/

a disappointing or insignificant occurrence that was expected to be important

Example: The party was a nonevent; people hardly came.

nook /ˈnʊk/

a secluded or sheltered place

Example: We found a seat in a little nook and had some lunch.

noose /ˈnus/

a loop in the end of a rope, tied with a slipknot, such as one used to hang people

Example: They had slid the noose from their necks and freed themselves of him.

norm /ˈnɔrm/

a standard that is required or regarded as normal

Example: The recent pattern of weather deviates from the norm for this time of year.

north /ˈnɔrθ/

one of the four cardinal points of the compass, at $0°$ or $360°$

Example: A compass needle always points north.

nose /ˈnoʊz/

the organ situated above the mouth, used for smelling and breathing

Example: He broke his nose in the fight.

nostril /ˈnɑstrɪl/

either of the two opening at the end of the nose

Example: Use your finger to press one nostril closed.

notation /noʊˈteɪʃən/

representation of numbers or quantities in a system by a series of symbols

Example: Using binary notation is in fact just manipulating ones and noughts.

note /nˈoʊt/
a brief informal note
Example: Just a quick note to wish you luck.
brief record in writing for future references
Example: Note down her telephone number in case you forget.
a critical comment or explanation in a book
Example: The tutor took note of her behavior.

notebook /nˈoʊtbʊk/
a book for writing in
Example: He drew out his notebook and began to take notes.

nothingness /ˈnəθɪŋnəs/
total insignificance
Example: I peered out into what seemed like nothingness.

notice /ˈnoʊtəs/
observation or attention
Example: He hardly seemed to notice my presence.
advance notification of something such as intention to end a contract of employment
Example: The tenant received two months' notice.

notification /ˌnoʊtəfəˈkeɪʃən/
the act of notifying someone of something
Example: We received official notification that Harry was missing.

notion /ˈnoʊʃən/
an idea or opinion
Example: I have only a vague notion of what she does for a living.

noun /ˈnaʊn/
a word that refers to a person, place, or thing
Example: "Sheep" is both a singular and plural noun.

novel /ˈnɑvəl/

a long fictional story in a book form

Example: Her latest novel is eagerly awaited.

novelist /ˈnɑvələst/

a writer of novels

Example: V.S. Naipaul is debatably the greatest novelist in history.

novelty /ˈnɑvəlti/

the quality of being new and interesting

Example: There's a certain novelty value in this approach.

novice /ˈnɑvəs/

a person who has entered a religion but has not yet taken vows

Example: As a novice writer, this is something I am interested in.

nuance /ˈnuɔns/

a subtle difference, as in colour, meaning, or tone

Example: He was aware of every nuance in her voice.

nucleus /ˈnukliəs/

the positively charged centre of an atom, made of protons and neutrons, about which electrons orbit

Example: The nucleus of an atom consists of neutrons, protons, and other particles

the part of the cell that contains the chromosomes and associated molecules that control the characteristics and growth of the cell

Example: DNA is stored in the nucleus of a cell.

a fundamental group of atoms in a molecule serving as the base structure for related compounds

Example: The nucleus of a deuterium atom contains a proton and a neutron.

nugget /ˈnʌgɪt/

a small lump of gold in its natural state

Example: You must find five or more gold nuggets to qualify for a cash prize.

nuisance /ˈnjusəns/

a person or thing that causes annoyance or bother

Example: He was a boring nuisance, and I'm glad to be rid of him.

number /nˈʌmbɚ/

a concept of quantity that is or can be derived from a single unit, a sum of units, or zero

Example: These plants produce a number of thin roots.

numeral /ˈnumɝəl/

a word or symbol used to express a sum or quantity

Example: A deputy stands guard under the black numeral 2.

numerator /ˈnuməˌreɪtɚ/

the number above the line in a fraction

Example: The numerator of the fraction is an integer.

numerology /numɝˈɑlədʒi/

the study of numbers and of their supposed influence on human affairs

Example: He studied numerology in the University.

numismatics /ˌnumɪsˈmætɪks/

the study or collection of coins or medals

Example: He is the only numismatics in the community.

nurse /ˈnʌs/

a person trained to look after sick people, usually in a hospital

Example: The young nurse was assisting at her first operation.

nursery /ˈnɝsɝi/

a room in a house where children sleep or play

Example: Anne tidied up the nursery.

nurture /nˈʌːtʃɚ/

the act or process of promoting the development of a child or young plant

Example: She wants to stay at home and nurture her children.

nut /ˈnət/

a dry one-seeded fruit that grows inside a hard shell

Example: He cracked his nut on the ceiling.

a small piece of metal with a hole in it, that screws on to a bolt

Example: The nut is not tight enough yet: give it another screw.

nutcracker /ˈnʌtˌkrækɚ/

a device for cracking the shells of nuts

Example: Clara receives a nutcracker, shaped like a toy soldier.

nutmeg /ˈnʌtˌmɛg/

a spice made from the seed of a tropical tree

Example: Sometimes I added a few gratings of nutmeg.

nutrient /ˈnutriənt/

a substance that provides nourishment

Example: The nutrient in the soil acts as a stimulus to growth to make the plants grow.

nutrition /nuˈtrɪʃən/

the process of taking in and absorbing nutrients

Example: Good nutrition is essential if patients are to make a quick recovery.

Oo

oak /ˈoʊk/

a large forest tree with hardwood, acorns as fruits, and leaves with a rounded projection

Example: The squirrel scurried up the trunk of the oak.

oarsman /ˈɔrzmən/

a person who rows

Example: The oarsman rowed vigorously, propelling the boat across the calm lake.

oasis /oʊˈeɪsɪs/

a fertile patch in a desert

Example: The explorers discovered a lush oasis in the middle of the Sahara Desert.

a place or situation offering relief during difficulty

Example: After a long and tiring day at work, my cosy home is a welcomed oasis.

oat /ˈoʊt/

a hard cereal grew as food

Example: The oat crop is mainly cultivated in temperate and subtropical countries.

oath /ˈoʊθ/

a solemn promise, especially to tell the truth in a court of law

Example: When testifying in court, the witness took an oath to tell the truth, the whole truth, and nothing but the truth.

an offensive or blasphemous expression

Example: She vented her anger with a torrent of oaths.

oatmeal /ˈoʊtˌmil/

a coarse flour made by grinding oats

Example: Oatmeal makes a healthy breakfast.

obeisance /oʊˈbeɪsəns/

an attitude or humble obedience

Example: The student showed obeisance to the teacher by standing up when he entered the classroom and waited for his permission to sit down.

obituary /oʊˈbɪtʃuˌɛri/

a published announcement of a death, usually with a short biography of the dead person

Example: The local newspaper published an obituary for a well-respected community leader who had passed away.

object /ˈɔːbd͡ʒɛkt/

a thing that can be touched or seen

Example: The police officer found a suspicious object in the abandoned building and immediately called for backup.

an aim or purpose

Example: The object of the game is to score more points than your opponent by shooting the ball into the hoop.

objection /əbˈdʒɛkʃən/

an expression or feeling of opposition or disapproval

Example: The teacher expressed her objection to the new English Literature curriculum.

objective /əbˈdʒɛktɪv/

an aim or purpose

Example: The teacher explained the objective of the lesson was to teach students how to write a persuasive essay.

objectivity /ɒbdʒɪktˈɪvɪti/

the quality of being objective

Example: Many people questioned the selection committee's objectivity.

obligation /ˌɑːblɪɡˈeɪʃən/

a moral or legal duty

Example: The company has an obligation to provide a safe working environment for its employees.

oblivion /əˈblɪviən/

the condition of being forgotten or disregarded

Example: The old building was left to rot and decay, slowly fading into oblivion over time.

obloquy /ˈɒbləˌkwi/

abusive statements or blame

Example: The politician endured years of obloquy after his controversial remarks.

oboe /ˈoʊboʊ/

a double-reeded woodwind instrument with a penetrating nasal tone

Example: My friend is a skilled oboe player and practices every day.

observance /əbˈzɜ-vəns/

the observing of law or custom

Example: The observance of social distancing guidelines is important to prevent the spread of disease.

observation /ˌɑbzɚˈveɪʃən/

the act of watching or the state of being watched

Example: The author's observation of human behaviour inspired his writing.

detailed examination of something before analysis, diagnosis, or interpretation

Example: The scientist made a detailed observation of the specimen under the microscope and realized that it was a new discovery.

obsession /əbˈsɛʃən/

something that preoccupies a person to the exclusion of other things

Example: She had an obsession with collecting vintage clothing.

obstacle /ˈɔbstəkəɫ/

a situation or event that prevents something from being done

Example: The language barrier proved to be a significant obstacle for international students.

obstetrician /ˌɔbstəˈtrɪʃən/

a doctor who specializes in pregnancy and childbirth

Example: The expectant mother went to see her obstetrician for a routine prenatal check-up.

obstruction /əbˈstrəkʃən/

a person or thing that obstructs

Example: The fallen tree created an obstruction in the road that caused traffic to back up for miles.

obstructionist /əbˈstrəkʃənəst/

a person who deliberately obstructs legal or parliamentary business

Example: The supervisor had to deal with an obstructionist employee who refused to follow company policies and procedures.

obverse /əbˈvɝs/

a counterpart or opposite

Example: The obverse side of the document had the official stamp and signature.

occasion /əˈkeɪʒən/

a particular event or the time at which it happens

Example: Her graduation was a momentous occasion, with friends and family gathering to celebrate her achievements.

a suitable time or opportunity to do something

Example: The stormy weather provided the perfect occasion to stay at home and catch up on some reading.

occupancy /ˈɔkjəpənsi/

the act of occupying a property

Example: The occupancy of the office space was low, as many employees were working remotely due to the pandemic.

occupant /ˈɔkjəpənt/

a person occupying a property

Example: The car's previous occupant left her phone behind.

occupation /ˌɔkjəˈpeɪʃən/

a person's job or profession

Example: His occupation was a doctor, and he loved helping people.

any activity on which someone's time is spent

Example: Her favourite occupation is reading books in her free time.

occupier /ˈɔkjəˌpaɪɚ/

the person who lives in a particular house, whether as owner or tenant

Example: The occupier of the apartment complex above mine was arrested by the police for noise nuisance.

occurrence /əˈkɝəns/

something that happens

Example: The frequent occurrence of power outages led to the installation of a generator.

ocean /ˈoʊʃən/

the vast area of salt water covering about 70 per cent of the earth's surface

Example: The ship sailed across the ocean for days before reaching its destination.

oceanography /ˌoʊʃəˈnɑgrəfi/

the study of oceans and their environment

Example: Oceanography is important for studying marine life and aquatic ecosystems.

octane /ˈɑkteɪn/

a liquid hydrocarbon found in petroleum

Example: I always fill up my car with high-octane gasoline to keep my engine running smoothly.

octave /ˈɑktɪv/

the musical interval between the first note and the eighth note of a major or minor scale

Example: The singer hit a high octave during the chorus of the song, and it gave the audience chills.

octet /ɔkˈtɛt/

a group of eight instrumentalists or singers

Example: The group of musicians formed an octet and performed a beautiful rendition of a classical piece.

octogenarian /ˌɔktədʒɪˈnɛɹiən/

a person between 80 and 89 years old

Example: My great-grandfather is an octogenarian, and he still goes for a walk every day to keep himself active.

octopus /ˈɔktəˌpʊs/

a sea creature with a soft oval body and eight long tentacles with suckers

Example: The octopus is a fascinating creature with eight arms and a highly intelligent brain.

oddity /ˈɔdəti/

an odd person or thing

Example: My neighbour is a bit of an oddity. He always wears mismatched flip-flops and carries a small plant everywhere he goes.

offence /oˈfɛns/

breaking of a law or rule

Example: The police officer charged him with the offence of driving without a license.

a cause of annoyance or anger

Example: His constant interrupting was an offence to the speaker and the rest of the audience.

offering /ˈɔfɚɪŋ/

something that is offered

Example: The company made an offering of its stock to the public to raise funds.

office /ˈɔːfɪs/

a room, set of rooms, or building in which business, professional duties, or clerical work are carried out

Example: She works in a small office with a team of five other people.

officer /ˈɔfəsɚ/

a person in the armed services, or on a non-naval ship, who holds a position of authority

Example: The army officer gave orders to his troops to prepare for the upcoming battle.

a person holding a position of authority in a government or organization

Example: The immigration officer checked my passport and visa before allowing me to enter the country.

offspring /ˈɔfsprɪŋ/

the immediate descendant or descendants of a person or animal

Example: My sister has three offspring, two sons and a daughter.

ogre /ˈoʊgɚ/

any monstrous or cruel person

Example: The boss was such an ogre that he made his employees work overtime without pay.

oil /ˈɔɪl/

any of a number of viscous liquids with a smooth sticky feel, which is usually flammable, insoluble in water, and is obtained from plants, animals, or mineral deposits by synthesis

Example: The oil spill in the ocean caused severe damage to the marine ecosystem.

oilfield /ˈɔɪlˌfiɫd/

an area containing reserves of oil

Example: The discovery of a new oilfield in the desert led to a rush of investors and developers.

ointment /ˈɔɪntmənt/

a smooth greasy substance applied to the skin to heal or protect, or as a cosmetic

Example: The mother used an ointment on her baby's diaper rash to soothe the irritated skin.

olive /ˈɑləv/

the small green or black bitter-tasting fruit of an evergreen Mediterranean tree

Example: I love to eat olives as a snack, especially the green ones stuffed with pimentos.

omelette /ˈɔmɫət/

a dish of beaten eggs cooked in a flat pan and often folded round a savoury filling

Example: The omelette I had for breakfast was delicious.

omen /ˈomən/

a thing or occurrence regarded as a sign of future happiness or disaster

Example: Seeing a black cat crossing your path is considered by some to be a bad omen.

omission /oˈmɪʃən/

something that has been left out or passed over

Example: The student received a lower grade due to the omission of key details in his essay.

onslaught /ˈɔnˌslɔt/

a violent attack

Example: The army launched an intense onslaught against the enemy's position.

ontology /ɑnˈtɔlədʒi/

the study of the nature of being

Example: Due to Rick's profound interest in human existence, he has chosen ontology as his major.

opacity /oʊˈpæsəti/

the state or quality of being opaque

Example: The opacity of the curtains blocked the sunlight from entering the room.

opal /ˈoʊpəl/

a precious stone, usually milky or bluish in colour, with shimmering changing reflections

Example: My best friend gifted me a beautiful opal necklace and ring for my birthday.

opening /ˈoʊpənɪŋ/

the beginning or first part of something

Example: The opening of the new science fiction movie was so captivating that I could not take my eyes off the screen.

opera /ˈɔprə/

a dramatic work in which most or all of the text is sung to orchestral accompaniment

Example: My Literature professor is a big fan of opera and often attends performances at the local theatre.

operation /ˌɔːpɚˈeɪʃən/

the act or method of operating

Example: The operation of the public transportation system was disrupted due to severe flooding.

a surgical procedure carried out to remove, replace, or repair a diseased or damaged part of the body

Example: My uncle is recovering well after the heart operation he had last week.

any procedure in which a number is derived from another number or numbers by applying specific rules

Example: In Mathematics class, we learned how to perform operations like addition, subtraction, multiplication, and division.

opinion /əpˈɪniən/

belief not founded on certainty or proof but on what seems probable

Example: In my opinion, this is the best restaurant in Rose Hall town for Chinese food.

opportunity /ɔːpɚˈtuːnɪri/

a favourable combination of circumstances

Example: I missed the opportunity to buy that designer dress when it was on sale.

orange /ˈɔrɪndʒ/

a round reddish-yellow juicy citrus fruit

Example: I always pack an orange in my lunch as a healthy and tasty afternoon snack.

a colour between red and yellow

Example: *I wore an orange dress to the party to stand out and make a statement*

orchestra /ˈɔːrkɪstrə/

a large group of musicians whose members play a variety of different instruments

Example: *The orchestra sounded magnificent during the symphony concert last evening.*

order /ˈɔːrdɚ/

an instruction that must be obeyed

Example: *The police officer gave an order for the driver to pull over to the side of the road.*

a state in which everything is arranged logically, comprehensibly, or naturally

Example: *The professor organized the lecture in a clear order, starting with the basics and building up to more advanced concepts.*

an established or customary system of society

Example: *The royal family follows a strict order of succession, determining who will become the next monarch.*

organization /ˌɔːrɡənɪˈzeɪʃən/

an organized group of people, such as a club, society, union, or business

Example: *My friend is starting her own organization to help promote local artists and creatives.*

the structure and arrangement of the different parts of something

Example: *The organization of the book's chapters make it easy to follow the author's arguments.*

outcome /ˈaʊtkʌm/

the result or consequence of something

Example: *The outcome of the election was a surprise to many people, as the polls had predicted a different result.*

outside /aʊtsˈaɪd/

the external side or surface of something

Example: The outside of the house needs a fresh coat of paint.

oven /ˈʌvən/

an enclosed heated compartment or container for baking or roasting food, or for drying or firing ceramics

Example: My grandmother always preheated the oven before putting the cake batter inside.

owner /ˈoʊnɚ/

a person who owns something

Example: He became the proud owner of a brand-new Rolls-Royce.

ox /ˈɔːks/

a castrated bull used for pulling heavy loads and for meat

Example: The farmer used an ox to plough his rice fields.

oxen /ˈɔːksən/

two or more castrated bulls used for pulling heavy loads and for meat

Example: The wagon was too heavy to be pulled by a horse, so the farmer used a pair of oxen instead.

Pp

pack /pˈak/

a group of animals that hunt together

Example: The hunters took precautions when they noticed a pack of wolves following them.

a complete set of playing cards

Example: The magician skillfully shuffled the pack of cards, mesmerizing the audience with his card tricks.

page /pˈeɪdʒ/

one side of one of the leaves of a book, newspaper, or magazine

Example: The newspaper article was printed on the front page, capturing the attention of readers.

a youth employed to run errands for the guests in a hotel or club

Example: The hotel hired a page to assist guests with their luggage and escort them to their rooms.

a small boy who attends a bride at her wedding

Example: The page held the bride's train as she made her way down the aisle, ensuring it flowed gracefully behind her.

pain /pˈeɪn/

physical hurt or discomfort caused by injury or illness

Example: The persistent pain in his lower back prompted him to seek the advice of a physical therapist.

emotional suffering

Example: The loss of a loved one can bring immense pain and grief, affecting one's emotional well-being.

paint /pˈeɪnt/

a coloured substance, spread on a surface with a brush or a roller, that forms a hard coating

Example: The artist carefully selected different shades of paint to create a vibrant and expressive painting.

painting /pˈeɪntɪŋ/

a picture produced by using paint

Example: The artist carefully mixed different colours of paint on her palette before applying them to the canvas.

pancake /pˈaŋkeɪk/

a thin flat circle of fried batter

Example: My mother makes the best pancakes.

panel /pˈanəl/

a distinct section of a large surface area, such as that in a door

Example: The front door of the house had an elegant wooden panel with intricate carvings.

a group of people acting as a team, such as in a quiz or a discussion before an audience

Example: The expert panel consisting of renowned scientists and researchers discussed the latest advancements in technology during the conference.

paper /pˈeɪpɚ/

a flexible material made in sheets from wood pulp or other fibres and used for writing on, decorating walls, wrapping parcels, etc.

Example: She reached for a sheet of paper from the stack on her desk and started jotting down notes for her upcoming presentation.

part /pˈɑːrt/

a piece or portion

Example: She took a small part of the cake and savoured its rich chocolate flavour.

an involvement in or contribution to something

Example: He played a significant part in the success of the company.

partnership /pˈɑːtnəʃˌɪp/

a relationship in which two or more people or organizations work together in a business venture

Example: The legal firm established a partnership with an accounting firm to offer comprehensive services to their clients, including legal and financial advice.

party /pˈɑːti/

a social gathering for pleasure

Example: We attended a costume party and had a great time seeing everyone's creative outfits.

a group of people sharing a common political aim

Example: The opposition party criticized the government's economic policies during the parliamentary debate.

passenger /pˈæsɪndʒɚ/

a person travelling in a vehicle operated by someone else

Example: The flight attendant welcomed the passengers aboard the plane and directed them to their seats.

passion /pˈæʃən/

any strongly felt emotion

Example: She pursued her passion for photography, capturing spectacular moments and conveying emotions through her images.

patience /pˈeɪʃəns/

the capacity for calmly enduring difficult situations

Example: The hiker's patience was rewarded when, after a long and strenuous climb, they reached the breath-taking summit with panoramic views.

the ability to wait calmly for something to happen without complaining or giving up

Example: Despite facing setbacks and obstacles, he maintained his patience and persevered in pursuing his dream career.

patron /pˈeɪtrən/

a person who financially supports artists, writers, musicians, or charities

Example: The orchestra's performances were made possible by the generous patrons who donated to ensure the continuation of their musical endeavours.

a regular customer of a shop, hotel, etc.

Example: The café welcomed its loyal patrons with warm smiles and personalized service, knowing their preferences and favourite orders.

payment /pˈeɪmənt/

the act of paying

Example: The customer provided their credit card information for the payment of the hotel reservation.

something given in return; punishment or reward

Example: The criminal faced a harsh payment for their actions, receiving a lengthy prison sentence.

peacock /pˈiːkɔːk/

a large male bird of the pheasant family with a crested head and a very large fanlike tail with blue and green eyelike spots

Example: In the zoo, visitors gathered around the peacock enclosure, fascinated by the elegant beauty of the birds.

a vain strutting person

Example: The party was filled with peacocks, boasting about their accomplishments, and seeking attention from others.

peer /pˈɪr/

a member of a nobility

Example: The king granted titles of nobility to his loyal subjects, elevating them to the ranks of peers.

a person of equal social standing

Example: She preferred to surround herself with peers who shared her passion for art and creativity.

penalty /pˈɛnəlti/

a legal punishment for a crime or offence

Example:　　The driver was given a penalty for running a red light.

loss or suffering because of one's own action

Example:　　She experienced the penalty of procrastination when she had to rush to complete her project at the last minute.

a handicap awarded against a player or team for illegal play

Example:　　The team was given a penalty for excessive roughness, resulting in the opposing team gaining a significant advantage.

pence /pˈɛns/

(plural) British bronze coins worth one-hundredth of a pound

Example:　　The cashier counted the pence carefully before handing over the correct change to the customer.

penny /pˈɛni/

(singular) British bronze coin worth one-hundredth of a pound

Example:　　She found a shiny penny on the sidewalk and picked it up for good luck.

people /pˈiːpəl/

persons collectively or in general

Example:　　People from all walks of life attended the concert, united by their love for music.

percentage /pɚsˈɛntɪdʒ/

proportion or rate per hundred parts

Example:　　The teacher announced the percentage of students who passed the exam.

perception /pɚsˈɛpʃən/

insight or intuition

Example:　　Her perception of the situation allowed her to understand the underlying motives and dynamics at play.

a way of viewing

Example: His perception of success was based on financial wealth and material possessions.

performance /pɚˈfɔrməns/

the act or process of performing

Example: The ballet performance was mesmerizing, with the dancers gracefully moving across the stage.

period /pˈiərɪəd/

a portion of time specified in some way

Example: The Jurassic period is known for its diverse and magnificent dinosaurs.

permission /pɚmˈɪʃən/

authorization to do something

Example: He asked his boss for permission to take a day off work to attend a family event.

person /pˈɜːsən/

an individual human being

Example: The person sitting next to me in the theatre was talking loudly throughout the entire movie.

personality /pˌɜːsənˈælɪti/

the distinctive characteristics which make an individual unique

Example: She has a charismatic personality that easily attracts people.

perspective /pɚspˈɛktɪv/

a way of regarding situations or facts and judging their relative importance

Example: From my perspective, the issue at hand requires immediate attention and action.

philosophy /fɪlˈɑːsəfi/

the academic study of knowledge thought, and the meaning of life

Example: She decided to major in philosophy to delve deeper into the fundamental questions about existence and human consciousness.

any system of beliefs or values

Example: The teacher's philosophy on education focused on fostering creativity, critical thinking, and a love for lifelong learning.

phone /fˈoʊn/

a piece of equipment for transmitting speech, consisting of a microphone and receiver mounted on a handset

Example: She picked up the phone and dialed her friend's number, eager to share the exciting news.

photo /fˈoʊroʊ/

a picture made by the chemical action of light on sensitive film

Example: She carefully placed the photo of her new-born baby in a beautiful frame on the mantelpiece.

photocopy /fˈoʊtəkˌɑːpi/

a photographic reproduction of written, printed, or graphic work

Example: The office had a dedicated photocopy machine for employees to reproduce documents as needed.

physics /fˈɪzɪks/

the branch of science concerned with the properties of matter and energy and the relationships between them

Example: He studied physics in college, fascinated by the laws that govern the universe and the fundamental principles of nature.

piano /piˈænoʊ/

a musical instrument played by depressing keys that cause hammers to strike strings and produce audible vibrations

Example: The family gathered around the piano, singing together, and enjoying the harmonious tunes.

picture /pˈɪktʃɚ/

a visual representation produced on a surface, such as in a photograph or painting

Example: The picture on the wall captured a serene landscape with vibrant colours.

a mental image

Example: The author's vivid descriptions created a beautiful picture in my mind of the enchanting forest.

a person or thing resembling another

Example: The new employee is a picture of professionalism, always impeccably dressed and composed.

pie /pˈaɪ/

a sweet or savoury filling baked in pastry

Example: She baked a delicious apple pie for dessert.

piece /pˈiːs/

a separate bit or part

Example: The carpenter measured and cut a piece of wood to fit perfectly into the frame.

pile /pˈaɪl/

a collection of objects laid on top of one another

Example: The books on my desk formed a tall pile, making it difficult to find what I was looking for.

a long heavy beam driven into the ground as a foundation for a structure

Example: The house was built on top of concrete piles to prevent it from sinking into the soft soil.

the fibres in a fabric that stand up or out from the weave

Example: The carpet had a plush pile that felt soft and comfortable underfoot.

pizza /pˈiːtsə/

a dish of Italian origin consisting of a baked disc of dough covered with a wide variety of savoury toppings

Example: They sat around the table, eagerly devouring the hot and cheesy pizza slices.

place /plˈeɪs/

a particular part of a space or of a surface

Example: I need to find a place in my room for my new shoe collection.

a geographical point, such as a town or city

Example: The beach is my favourite place to relax and unwind.

house or living quarters

Example: Our new place is a cosy apartment with a spacious living room.

right or duty

Example: As a citizen, it is our place to vote and participate in the democratic process.

plan /plˈɑn/

a method thought out for doing or achieving something

Example: She devised a detailed plan to renovate her house, outlining each step of the process.

a detailed drawing to scale of a horizontal section through a building

Example: The architect presented the plan of the new office building, showing the layout of each floor and the placement of rooms.

an outline or sketch

Example: Before writing the essay, she created a plan to organize her thoughts and structure her arguments.

platform /plˈɑtfɔːm/

a raised area at a railway station where passengers get on or off the train

Example: She stood on the platform, waiting for her friend to arrive on the next train.

the declared aims of a political party

Example: The political party's platform emphasized its commitment to economic reform and social justice.

player /plˈeɪɚ/

a person who takes part in a game or sport

Example: The chess player carefully analyzed the board, strategizing his moves to outwit his opponent.

a person who plays a musical instrument

Example: The drummer is known for being an energetic and dynamic player, driving the rhythm of the band.

poem /pˈoʊəm/

a literary work, often in verse, usually dealing with emotional or descriptive themes in a rhythmic form

Example: She wrote a heartfelt poem as a tribute to her late grandmother, expressing her love and grief.

poet /pˈoʊɛt/

a writer of poetry

Example: Emily Dickinson is widely regarded as a brilliant poet whose work continues to inspire readers today.

poetry /pˈoʊɛtri/

the art or craft of writing poems

Example: The poetry workshop was attended by aspiring writers who wanted to improve their poetic skills.

a poetic quality that prompts an emotional response

Example: Her dance had a graceful poetry to it, captivating the audience and evoking a sense of wonder.

point /pˈɔɪnt/

the essential idea in an argument or discussion

Example: She made a compelling point during the debate, shedding light on an important aspect of the issue.

a reason or aim

Example: The point of this discussion is to help you understand my concerns.

a location or position

Example: The hikers reached the highest point of the mountain trail.

police /pəlˈiːs/

the organized civil force in a state which keeps law and order

Example: The police arrived at the scene of the accident to assess the situation and ensure the safety of those involved.

policeman /pəlˈiːsmən/

a member of a police force

Example: The policeman issued a ticket to the driver for exceeding the speed limit.

policy /pˈɑːlɪsi/

a plan of action adopted by a person, group, or government

Example: The school has a zero-tolerance policy for bullying, promoting a safe and inclusive environment.

a document containing an insurance contract

Example: Before signing up for car insurance, make sure to carefully review the policy to understand the coverage and terms.

politics /pˈɔːlətˌɪks/

the art and science of government

Example: She studied politics in college to gain a deeper understanding of how governments function.

any activity concerned with the acquisition of power

Example: The corporate world can sometimes be dominated by office politics, where individuals vie for power and influence.

pollution /pəlˈuːʃən/

harmful or poisonous substances introduced into an environment

Example: The pollution caused by plastic waste has become a global concern, affecting marine life and ecosystems.

population /pˌɔːpjʊlˈeɪʃən/

all the inhabitants of a place

Example: The population of the city has been steadily growing over the past decade.

position /pəzˈɪʃən/

place or location

Example: He found a comfortable position on the couch and settled in to watch a movie.

the way in which a person or thing is placed or arranged

Example: The photographer asked the model to change her position slightly to capture the best angle for the photo.

possession /pəzˈɛʃən/

the state of owning or having

Example: Her most cherished possession is a family heirloom passed down through generations.

possibility /pˌɑːsəbˈɪlɪti/

the state of being possible

Example: The weather forecast indicated a possibility of rain later in the day.

post /pˈoʊst/

an official system of mail delivery

Example: I dropped the package off at the post this morning to send it to my friend.

a length of wood, metal, or concrete fixed upright to support or mark something

Example: The sign was mounted on a sturdy metal post at the entrance of the park.

pot /pˈɔːt/

a round deep container, often with a handle and a lid, used for cooking

Example: The chef stirred the soup in the large pot, ensuring all the flavours melded together perfectly.

potato /pəˈeɪtoʊ/

a starchy vegetable that grows underground

Example: The farmer harvested a bountiful crop of potatoes from his field.

power /pˈaʊɚ/

ability to do something

Example: She knew she had the power to overcome her depression.

political, financial, or social force or authority

Example: The government wields significant power in making decisions that affect the nation and its citizens.

a person or group having authority

Example: Our boss had to answer to the higher power for his behaviour and was disciplined accordingly.

practice /prˈæktɪs/

something done frequently or repeatedly

Example: Reading is a practice that enriches the mind and broadens one's knowledge and perspective.

the business or surgery of a lawyer or doctor

Example: The lawyer's practice specializes in criminal defence, representing clients accused of various offences.

preference /prˈɛfrəns/

a liking for one thing above the rest

Example: When it comes to food, his preference is for spicy cuisine with bold flavours.

preparation /prˌɛpɚˈeɪʃən/

the act of preparing or being prepared

Example: The chef began the preparation of the meal by gathering all the necessary ingredients and organizing them in the kitchen.

presence /prˈɛzəns/

the fact of being in a specified place

Example: Her presence at the meeting was essential as she had valuable insights to contribute to the discussion.

impressive personal appearance or bearing

Example: Her mere presence commands attention.

presentation /ˌprɛzənˈteɪʃən/

the act of presenting or being presented

Example: The speaker captivated the audience with an engaging presentation on climate change.

a formal ceremony in which an award is made

Example: The graduation ceremony concluded with the presentation of diplomas to the graduating students.

president /prˈɛzɪdənt/

the head of state of a republic

Example: The president delivered a powerful speech addressing the nation's current challenges and outlining plans.

the head of a company, society, or institution

Example: The president of the company oversees the overall operations and strategic direction of the organization.

a person who presides over a meeting

Example: The president called the meeting to order and welcomed all attendees.

pressure /prˈɛʃɚ/

the state of pressing or being pressed

Example: He felt immense pressure to succeed and meet the high expectations set by his family.

the application of force by one body on the surface of another

Example: The massage therapist applied gentle pressure to the client's muscles to release tension.

price /prˈaɪs/

the amount of money for which a thing is bought or sold

Example: The price of gasoline has been steadily increasing, causing concern among motorists.

priest /prˈiːst/

a minister of any religion

Example: The priest delivered a powerful sermon that touched the hearts of the congregation.

principle /prˈɪnsɪpəl/

a moral rule guiding personal conduct

Example: Honesty is a fundamental principle that guides my actions and interactions with others.

priority /praɪˈɔːrɪti/

the most important thing that must be dealt with first

Example: The safety of students takes priority over any other matter.

the right to be or go before others

Example: Playing cricket was not high on my list of priorities.

problem /prɔːbləm/

someone or something that is difficult to deal with

Example: Stress is a major problem in modern life.

a puzzle or question set for solving

Example: There is no obvious solution to that mathematical problem.

procedure /prəsˈiːdʒɚ/

a way of doing something

Example: The company has a strict procedure in place for handling customer complaints.

process /prˈɑːsɛs/

a series of natural developments which result in an overall change

Example: The process of photosynthesis in plants involves the conversion of sunlight, water, and carbon dioxide into glucose and oxygen.

a method of doing or producing something

Example: The hiring process at the company includes application screening, interviews, and reference checks.

product /prɔːdʌkt/

something produced

Example: The factory produces a wide range of electronic products, including smartphones, laptops, and tablets.

a consequence

Example: The lack of communication between team members was a product of mismanagement and poor coordination.

profession /prəfˈɛʃən/

a type of work that requires special training, such as law or medicine

Example: The legal profession requires years of study and passing the bar exam to practice as a lawyer.

a declaration of a belief or feeling

Example: Her profession of love for him caught him by surprise, as he had no idea she felt that way.

professor /prəfˈɛsɚ/

the highest rank of teacher in a university

Example: The professor delivered an engaging lecture, captivating the students with her extensive knowledge and expertise.

profit /prˈɑːfɪt/

money gained in business or trade

Example: The entrepreneur started the business with the goal of making a profit and achieving financial stability.

a benefit or advantage

Example: One of the great profits of regular exercise is improved physical fitness and overall health.

program /prˈoʊgræm/

a sequence of coded instructions which enables a computer to perform various tasks

Example: The software engineer developed a program that automates data analysis and generates reports.

promotion /prəmˈoʊʃən/

activity that supports or encourages a cause, venture, or aim

Example: The school organized a fundraising promotion to support the construction of a new library.

the publicizing of a product, organization, or venture so as to increase sales or public awareness

Example: The smartphone company's promotion of its latest model resulted in a surge in sales.

property /prˈɑːpɚti/

something owned

Example: The couple purchased a beautiful waterfront property as their dream home.

Prophet /prɔːfɪt/

a person supposedly chosen by God to pass on His message

Example: The prophet's words resonated with the crowd, inspiring them to seek spiritual enlightenment and follow the divine teachings.

proposal /prəpˈoʊzəl/

a suggestion put forward for consideration

Example: The research team submitted a proposal to secure funding for their innovative study on renewable energy sources.

prospectus /prəspˈɛktəs/

booklet produced by a university, company, etc. giving details about it and its activities

Example: The company's prospectus outlined its business model, financial projections, and investment opportunities for potential investors.

protection /prət'ɛkʃən/

the act of protecting or the condition of being protected

Example: Wearing a helmet provides an extra layer of protection for cyclists, reducing the risk of head injuries in case of an accident.

psychology /saɪk'ɑːlədʒi/

the scientific study of all forms of human and animal behaviour

Example: She pursued a degree in psychology to gain a deeper understanding of human behaviour and mental processes.

puppy /p'ʌpi/

a young dog

Example: The puppy wagged its tail excitedly as it played with its favourite toy in the backyard.

purpose /p'ʌrːpəs/

the reason for which anything is done, created, or exists

Example: The purpose of the study was to investigate the effects of climate change on marine ecosystems.

determination

Example: With unwavering purpose, she pushed through the obstacles and challenges to achieve her dreams.

Qq

quadrant /ˈkwɑdrənt/

a quarter of the circumference of a circle

Example: We divided the circular cake into four equal quadrants to share among our friends.

an instrument formerly used in astronomy and navigation for measuring the altitudes of stars

Example: My grandfather showed me his antique quadrant, a fascinating instrument used by sailors to navigate the seas.

quadratic /kwɑˈdrɑtɪk/

an equation in which the variable is raised to the power of two, but nowhere raised to a higher power

Example: In math class, we learned how to solve quadratic equations using factoring or the quadratic formula.

quadriceps /ˈkwɑdrəˌsɛps/

a muscle at the front of the thigh

Example: After running a marathon, my quadriceps were sore and in need of some rest.

quagmire /ˈkwæɡˌmaɪɚ/

a soft wet area of land that gives way under the feet

Example: After heavy rain, the backyard turned into a quagmire, making it difficult to walk.

quail /ˈkweɪl/

a small game bird of the partridge family

Example: The hunters set out early in the morning in search of quail for their supper.

qualification /ˌkwɑləfəˈkeɪʃən/

an official record of achievement awarded on the successful completion of a course of training or passing of an examination

Example: Having a bachelor's degree is often seen as a basic qualification for many professional jobs.

qualifier /ˈkwɑləˌfaɪɚ/

a person or thing that qualifies, especially a contestant in a competition who wins a preliminary heat or contest and so earns the right to take part in the next round

Example: As the reigning champion, she was automatically granted a place as a qualifier in the final round.

quality /kwˈɔlɪti/

degree or standard of excellence

Example: The company's commitment to quality is reflected in the positive feedback from its customers.

quandary /ˈkwɑndɚi/

a situation in which it is difficult to decide what to do

Example: She found herself in a quandary when faced with the choice between pursuing her passion or taking a stable job.

quantity /kwˈɔntɪti/

a specified or definite amount or number

Example: The chef carefully measures the quantity of ingredients to ensure the recipe turns out perfectly.

quantum /ˈkwɑntəm/

an amount or quantity, especially a specific amount

Example: The success of the experiment hinged on finding the right quantum of the substance.

the smallest quantity of some physical property that a system can possess

Example: The scientist conducted experiments to measure the quantum of energy released during the reaction.

quarantine /ˈkwɔrənˌtin/

a period of isolation, especially of people or animals arriving from abroad, to prevent the spread of disease

Example: The government implemented a strict quarantine policy to contain the spread of the virus.

quark /ˈkwɑrk/

the hypothetical elementary particle supposed to be a fundamental unit of all baryons and mesons

Example: Scientists at the particle physics laboratory are studying the behaviour of quarks to better understand the fundamental building blocks of matter.

quarrel /ˈkwɔrəl/

an angry disagreement

Example: The quarrel between the neighbours started over a dispute about parking spaces.

quarry /ˈkwɔri/

a place where stone is dug from the surface of the earth

Example: The workers at the quarry use heavy machinery to extract rocks and minerals.

an animal that is being hunted

Example: The hunters tracked the movements of their quarry, hoping to get a successful shot.

quart /ˈkwɔrt/

a unit of liquid measure equal to one-quarter of a gallon or two pints (1.136 litres)

Example: She bought a quart of milk from the grocery store to use for her recipe.

quarter /ˈkwɔrtɚ/

one of four equal parts of something such as an object or quantity

Example: She took a quarter of the cake and saved the rest for later.

quarterback /ˈkwɔrtɚˌbæk/

a player in American football who directs attacking play

Example: The quarterback threw a long pass to his teammate, who caught it for a touchdown.

quarters /ˈkwɔrtɚz/

accommodation, especially as provided for military personnel

Example: The soldiers were assigned to their quarters, where they would be staying for the duration of their deployment.

quartet /kwɔrˈtɛt/

a group of four singers or instrumentalists

Example: The local jazz quartet is known for their energetic and captivating performances.

quartile /ˈkwɔrtɪl/

one of three values of a variable dividing its distribution into four groups with equal frequencies

Example: The sales data was divided into quartiles to determine the performance of different product categories.

quartz /ˈkwɔrts/

a hard glossy mineral consisting of crystalline silicon dioxide

Example: He collected various quartz crystals during his hiking trip in the mountains.

queen /kwˈiːn/

a female sovereign who is the official ruler or head of state

Example: The Queen attended a state dinner to welcome foreign dignitaries.

query /ˈkwiri/

a question, especially one expressing doubt

Example: The student approached the teacher after class with a query about the assignment.

quest /ˈkwɛst/

the object of search

Example: The hero embarked on a quest to find the lost treasure and restore peace to the kingdom.

question /kwˈɛstʃən/

a form of words addressed to a person in order to obtain an answer

Example: The detective asked the suspect a series of questions to gather information about the crime.

questionnaire /ˌkwɛstʃəˈnɛr/

a set of questions on a form, used to collect statistical information or opinions from people

Example: The company sent out a questionnaire to its customers to gather feedback on their satisfaction with the product.

queue /ˈkju/

a line of people or vehicles waiting for something

Example: The queue at the grocery store was quite long, but it moved quickly.

quiche /ˈkiʃ/

savoury flan with an egg custard filling to which cheese, bacon, or vegetables are added

Example: My mom makes the best quiche with a combination of ham, mushrooms, and Swiss cheese.

quicksand /ˈkwɪkˌsænd/

a deep mass of loose wet sand that submerges anything on top of it

Example: The children were warned to stay away from the quicksand at the beach for their safety.

quicksilver /ˈkwɪkˈsɪlvɚ/

the metal mercury

Example: The broken thermometer spilt quicksilver all over the floor.

quilt /ˈkwɪlt/

a cover for a bed, consisting of a soft filling sewn between two layers of material

Example: She snuggled up under the cosy quilt on a cold winter night.

quince /ˈkwɪns/

the acid-tasting pear-shaped fruit of an Asian tree, used in preserves

Example: I bought some quinces from the farmer's market to make homemade quince jam.

quintessence /kwɪnˈtɛsəns/

the most perfect representation of a quality or state

Example: The painting captured the quintessence of beauty, with its harmonious colours and delicate brushstrokes.

quintuplet /ˈkwɪnˈtəplət/

one of five children born at one birth

Example: My adopted aunt discovered that she is a quintuplet.

quiz /ˈkwɪz/

an entertainment in which the knowledge of the players is tested by a series of questions

Example: He won the quiz competition by correctly answering the final question.

quota /ˈkwoʊtə/

the share that is due from, due to, or allocated to a person or group

Example: Each team member was given a quota of sales to meet by the end of the month.

quotation /kwoʊˈteɪʃən/

an estimate of costs submitted by a contractor to a prospective client

Example: The contractor provided a detailed quotation for the construction project, outlining the estimated costs of materials and labour.

quotient /ˈkwoʊʃənt/

the result of the division of one number or quantity by another

Example: *The teacher asked the students to find the quotient of 56 divided by 8 as part of their math assignment.*

Rr

radio /rˈeɪdɪˌoʊ/

the use of electromagnetic waves for broadcasting or two-way communication without the use of linking wires

Example: The ship's crew relied on radio communication to stay connected with the coast guard and receive updates about weather conditions.

an electronic device for converting radio signals into sounds

Example: The radio played my favourite song as I drove down the highway.

radius /rˈeɪdɪəs/

a straight line joining the centre of a circle to any point on the circumference

Example: The engineer calculated the radius of the cylindrical pipe to ensure it would fit perfectly into the existing plumbing system.

raincoat /rˈeɪŋkoʊt/

a coat made of a waterproof material

Example: She put on her yellow raincoat and grabbed an umbrella before heading out into the rainy weather.

range /rˈeɪndʒ/

the distance between a target and a weapon

Example: The archer displayed incredible accuracy, hitting the bullseye from a range of 50 meters.

the limits within which a person or thing can function effectively

Example: The car's electric range was impressive, allowing drivers to travel up to 300 miles on a single charge.

the difference in pitch between the highest and lowest note of a voice or musical instrument

Example: The soprano singer had an impressive vocal range, effortlessly hitting both high and low notes with precision and clarity.

rate /rˈeɪt/

a quantity or amount considered in relation to or measured against another quantity or amount

Example: The success rate of the project was calculated to be 90%, indicating that it achieved a significant portion of its intended objectives.

a price or charge with reference to a standard or scale

Example: The hotel offered different room rates based on the amenities and size.

the speed of progress or change

Example: The rate at which technology is advancing is truly remarkable, with new innovations emerging almost every day.

ratio /rˈeɪʃɪˌoʊ/

the relationship between two or more numbers or amounts expressed as a proportion

Example: The recipe calls for a ratio of 2 cups of flour to 1 cup of sugar.

rattlesnake /rˈærəlsnˌeɪk/

a poisonous snake with loose horny segments on the tail that make a rattling sound

Example: The campers were advised to be mindful of their surroundings and watch out for any signs of rattlesnakes in the area.

reaction /rɪˈækʃən/

a physical or emotional response to a stimulus

Example: The medicine caused an allergic reaction, resulting in hives and difficulty breathing.

reality /rɪˈælɪri/

the state of things as they are or appear to be, rather than as one might wish them to be

Example: Despite his dreams of becoming a professional athlete, the reality was that he lacked the necessary skills and physical abilities.

reason /rˈiːzən/

a cause or motive for a belief or action

Example: The doctor explained the reason for the patient's symptoms.

reception /risˈɛpʃən/

an area in an office, hotel, etc. where visitors are received or reservations dealt with

Example: We waited patiently in the reception area for our appointment.

a formal party for guests

Example: The couple organized a lavish reception to celebrate their wedding.

the way something is received

Example: The novel's reception among readers was overwhelmingly positive.

recipe /rˈɛsɪpˌiː/

a list of ingredients and directions for making a particular dish

Example: The chef shared her secret recipe for the famous spaghetti sauce.

a method for achieving something

Example: The recipe for a successful career includes a combination of education, experience, and networking.

recognition /rˌɛkəgnˈɪʃən/

the act of recognizing

Example: The athlete received recognition for breaking the world record in the 100-meter sprint.

recommendation /ˌrɛkəmɛndˈeɪʃən/

a suggestion or proposal as to the best course of action

Example: The committee's recommendation to invest in renewable energy projects was approved.

record /ˈrɛkɚd/

information or data on a subject collected over a long period

Example: The company keeps a record of all financial transactions to ensure accurate accounting.

a thin disc of a plastic material upon which sound has been recorded in a continuous spiral groove on each side

Example: He carefully placed the needle on the record, and the room filled with the melodic tunes of his favourite song.

the known facts about a person's achievements

Example: The student's academic record demonstrated consistently high grades and participation in extracurricular activities.

a list of crimes of which an accused person has previously been convicted

Example: The court denied bail based on the defendant's extensive criminal record.

recording /rɪkˈɔːrdɪŋ/

something that has been recorded

Example: The audio recording of the lecture helped me review the material for the examination.

reflection /rɪflˈɛkʃən/

an image of an object given back in a mirror

Example: As I stood in front of the mirror, my reflection stared back at me, mirroring my every move.

careful or long considerations

Example: The professor encouraged the students to engage in deep reflection on the topic.

a transformation of a shape in which right and left, or top and bottom, are reversed

Example: The geometry lesson focused on teaching students about reflections and their impact on shapes.

refrigerator /rɪfrˈɪdʒərˌeɪtər/

a cabinet for keeping food and drink cool

Example: I need to go to the grocery store to restock the refrigerator with fresh produce and dairy products.

region /rˈiːdʒən/

an area considered as a unit for geographical or social reasons

Example: I grew up in a coastal region, where I spent my days enjoying the sandy beaches.

relation /rɪlˈeɪʃən/

the connection between things or people

Example: The relation between the two countries has improved significantly since they signed the peace treaty.

relationship /rɪlˈeɪʃənʃˌɪp/

the dealings and feelings that exist between people or groups

Example: Building a strong relationship requires trust, communication, and mutual respect.

association by blood or marriage

Example: The family tree provided a visual representation of the intricate relationships among generations.

relaxation /rɪlæksˈeɪʃən/

a form of recreation

Example: Taking a warm bath is one of my favourite methods of relaxation.

replacement /rɪplˈeɪsmənt/

the act or process of replacing a person or thing with another

Example: After the old computer broke down, they purchased a new one as a replacement.

republic /rɪpˈʌblɪk/

a form of government in which the people or their elected representatives possess the supreme power

Example: In a republic, the constitution serves as the foundation for governance and protects the rights of individuals.

reputation /ˌrɛpjuːˈteɪʃən/

the opinion generally held of a person or thing

Example: Her reputation as a trustworthy businesswoman attracted many investors to her new venture.

requirement /rɪkwˈaɪɚmənt/

something demanded or imposed as an obligation

Example: The job advertisement listed the specific requirements needed for the position.

research /risˈɜːtʃ/

systematic investigation to establish facts or collect information on a subject

Example: Her research into ancient civilizations shed light on their cultural practices and beliefs.

resolution /ˌrɛzəlˈuːʃən/

firmness or determination

Example: The team's resolution to succeed drove them to work tirelessly and achieve their goals.

resource /risˈoːrs/

something resorted to for is or support

Example: The internet has become an essential resource for accessing information and connecting with people worldwide.

the ability to deal with problems

Example: In times of crisis, her resilience and inner strength were her greatest resources.

response /rɪspˈɔːns/

a reply or reaction

Example: She smiled in response to his kind gesture.

responsibility /rɪspˌɑːnsəbˈɪlɪti/

the state of having control or authority over

Example: The manager delegated the responsibility of overseeing the project to a trusted team member.

restaurant /rˈɛstrɔːnt/

a place where meals are prepared and served to customers

Example: The restaurant offers a variety of vegan options to cater to customers with different dietary preferences.

result /rɪzˈʌlt/

the outcome or consequence of an action, policy, etc.

Example: The result of the experiment confirmed the hypothesis.

revenge /rˈɛvənˌuː/

something done as a means of vengeance

Example: The desire for revenge consumed him and led him down a path of destruction.

review /rɪvjˈuː/

a critical assessment of a book, film, etc.

Example: The movie received mixed reviews from critics, with some praising its performances while others criticized its plot.

revolution /rˌɛvəlˈuːʃən/

the overthrown of a regime or political system by the governed

Example: The French Revolution in the late 18th century led to the downfall of the monarchy and the rise of a republic.

a movement in or as if in a circle

Example: The wheels of the bicycle spun in constant revolution as the rider pedaled forward.

ringworm /rˈɪŋwʌːm/

a fungal infection of the skin producing itchy patches

Example: My cousin developed ringworm after playing with dirty water and had to get treatment from the doctor.

risk /rˈɪsk/

the possibility of bringing about misfortune or loss

Example: The decision to start a new business entailed both opportunities and risks.

river /rˈɪvɚ/

a large natural stream of fresh water flowing along a definite course into the sea, a lake, or a large river

Example: We went fishing by the river and caught some trout for our dinner.

road /rˈoʊd/

a route, usually surfaced, used by travellers and vehicles to get from one place to another

Example: The road was congested with traffic during rush hour, causing delays for commuters.

rock /rˈɔːk/

the mass of mineral matter that makes up part of the earth's crust

Example: The hiker stumbled upon a beautiful rock formation while exploring the mountain trail.

a person or thing on which one can always depend

Example: My mother has always been my rock.

roe /rˈoʊ/

the ovary and eggs of a female fish, sometimes eaten as food

Example: The market had a variety of roe available, including trout, sturgeon, and caviar.

a small, graceful deer with short antlers

Example: We were lucky to spot a group of roe grazing peacefully in the meadow.

role /rˈoʊl/

a task or function

Example: Her role in the project was to oversee the budget and financial aspects of the team's activities.

roof /rˈuːf/

a structure that covers or forms the top of a building or other structure

Example: The roof of the house was damaged during the storm, causing water to leak into the rooms below.

room /rˈuːm/

an area within a building enclosed by a floor, a ceiling, and walls

Example: The children rushed into the empty room, excited to have a space to play and run around.

unoccupied or unobstructed space

Example: Jack scooted over, creating room for Jenny to take a seat beside him.

rule /rˈuːl/

a customary form or procedure

Example: The school has a rule that students must always wear their uniforms.

the period in which a government has power

Example: The monarchy's rule lasted for several centuries.

a device with a straight edge for guiding or measuring

Example: The carpenter used a rule to ensure precise measurements when cutting the wood.

Ss

safety /sˈeɪfti/

the quality or state of being free from danger

Example: Safety should always be a top priority when operating heavy machinery.

salad /sˈæləd/

a dish of raw vegetables, often served with a dressing, eaten as a separate course or as part of a main course

Example: She enjoyed a refreshing salad of mixed greens, cherry tomatoes, and cucumbers for lunch.

salmon /sˈæmən/

a large pink-fleshed fish which is highly valued for food

Example: We enjoyed a delicious meal of baked salmon accompanied by roasted vegetables.

salt /sˈɔlt/

a white crystalline substance, used for seasoning and preserving food; sodium chloride

Example: The recipe called for a teaspoon of salt to enhance the taste of the soup.

sample /sˈæmpəl/

a small part of anything, taken as being representative of a whole

Example: The scientist took a water sample from the river to test its quality and contamination levels.

sandcastle /sˈɑndkæsəl/

a model of a castle made from sand

Example: They decorated their sandcastle with seashells and colourful flags to make it more enchanting.

sanity /sˈænɪti/

good sense or soundness of judgement

Example: The therapist helped her find her way back to sanity after experiencing a traumatic event.

satisfaction /sˌatɪsfˈækʃən/

the pleasure obtained from the fulfilment of a desire

Example: He felt a sense of satisfaction after completing a challenging project.

scale /skˈeɪl/

a machine or device for weighing

Example: The doctor asked the patient to step on the scale to measure her weight.

the ratio between the size of something real and that of a representation of it

Example: The map displayed a scale at the bottom, indicating the relationship between distances on the map and real-world distances.

scarf /skˈɑːrf/

a piece of material worn around the head, neck, or shoulders

Example: She wrapped a warm woolen scarf around her neck to protect herself from the cold winter wind.

scene /sˈiːn/

the place where an action or event, real or imaginary, occurs

Example: The crime scene was carefully examined by the forensic investigators for any evidence.

a division of an act of a play, in which the setting is fixed, and the action is continuous

Example: Act 2, Scene 3 of the play takes place in a cosy living room with the characters engaged in a heated argument.

school /skˈuːl/

a place where children are educated

Example: The children eagerly packed their backpacks and headed to school early in the morning.

a group of sea-living animals that swim together, such as fish, whales, or dolphins

Example: We were fortunate to witness a large school of dolphins playing and leaping out of the water.

science /sˈaɪəns/

the study of the nature and behaviour of the physical universe, based on observation, experiment, and measurement

Example: The science teacher engaged her students with hands-on experiments to foster their curiosity and critical thinking skills.

screen /skrˈiːn/

the blank surface on which visible images are formed or projected

Example: She glanced at the computer screen to read the email that just arrived.

secretary /sˈɛkrətri/

a person who handles correspondence, keeps records, and does general clerical work for an individual or organization

Example: He was hired as a secretary to assist the department with administrative tasks and document management.

section /sˈɛkʃən/

a part cut off or separated from the main body of something

Example: The book was divided into several sections, each covering a different topic.

sector /sˈɛktɚ/

a part or subdivision, especially of a society or an economy

Example: The healthcare sector plays a vital role in providing medical services and promoting public health.

either portion of a circle bounded by two radii and the arc cut off by them

Example: The circular cake was sliced into several sectors to ensure equal portions for all the guests.

security /sɪkjˈʊrɪti/

precautions taken to ensure against theft, espionage, or other danger

Example: The government implemented strict security protocols to safeguard classified information.

something given or pledged to guarantee payment of a loan

Example: The borrower provided his car as security for the loan he obtained from the bank.

selection /sɪlˈɛkʃən/

a range from which something may be selected

Example: The store offers a wide selection of clothing for customers to choose from.

self-control /sˈɛlf-kəntrˈoʊl/

the ability to control one's feelings, emotions, or reactions

Example: She relied on her self-control to resist the temptation of indulging in unhealthy snacks.

sense /sˈɛns/

a feeling perceived through one of the senses

Example: The spicy taste of the curry awakened her sense of taste, leaving a lingering flavour on her palate.

a mental perception or awareness

Example: He had a gut sense that something was off about the situation.

series /sˈɪriz/

a group or succession of related things

Example: The bookstore displayed a series of books by the same author on a dedicated shelf.

the sum of a finite or infinite sequence of numbers or quantities

Example: The mathematician derived the formula for the sum of an arithmetic series to calculate the total.

service /sˈʌrːvɪs/

an act of help or assistance

Example: The hotel staff provided excellent service.

a regular check made on a machine or vehicle in which parts are tested, cleaned, or replaced if worn

Example: The technician performed a routine service on the air conditioning unit, cleaning the filters, and checking for any issues.

session /sˈɛʃən/

any period devoted to a particular activity

Example: The therapy session provided a safe and confidential space for individuals to discuss their thoughts and emotions.

set /sˈɛt/

a number of objects or people grouped or belonging together

Example: The tool set contained a variety of wrenches, screwdrivers, and pliers for different repair tasks.

a television or piece of radio equipment

Example: The radio set allowed me to tune in to my favourite stations and enjoy music and talk shows.

setting /sˈɛtɪŋ/

the scenery, properties, or background used to create the location for a stage play or film

Example: The film crew spent days preparing the setting for the outdoor scene, arranging props, and creating a realistic landscape.

the plates and cutlery for a single place at a table

Example: The elegant table setting featured fine China plates, polished silver cutlery, and crystal glassware.

shape /ʃ eɪp/

the figure or outline of the body of a person

Example: The fashion industry celebrates diversity by featuring models of all shapes and sizes on the runway.

condition or state of efficiency

Example: The car's engine was in poor shape and required extensive repairs.

share /ʃ ɛr/

a part or portion of something that belongs to or is contributed by a person or group

Example: The group project required each member to contribute their fair share of work and ideas.

sheep /ʃ iːp/

a cud-chewing mammal with a thick woolly coat kept for its wool and meat

Example: The sheep peacefully grazed on the green meadow, enjoying the fresh grass.

shelf /ʃ ɛlf/

a board fixed horizontally against a wall or in a cupboard, for holding things

Example: The kitchen shelf was filled with spices, neatly arranged in alphabetical order for easy access.

a projecting layer of ice or rock on land or in the sea

Example: The research team studied the unique ecosystem thriving beneath the Antarctic ice shelf.

shepherd /ʃ ɛpɚd/

a person employed to tend sheep

Example: The shepherd guided the flock of sheep to the grazing field, ensuring their safety and well-being.

shirt /ʃ ʌrt/

an item of clothing worn on the upper part of the body, usually with a collar and sleeves and buttoning up the front

Example: He wore a crisp white shirt and a tie for the formal business meeting.

shoal /ʃoʊl/

a large group of fish swimming together

Example: The fishermen spotted a massive shoal of tuna and quickly cast their nets, hoping for a plentiful catch.

a sandbank or rocky area, especially one that can be seen at low water

Example: The children enjoyed playing on the shoal at the beach, collecting seashells and building sandcastles.

shower /ʃaʊɚ/

a kind of bathing in which a person stands upright and is sprayed with water from a nozzle

Example: After a long day at work, she enjoyed a relaxing shower to wash away the stress and refresh herself.

a brief period of rain, hail, sleet, or snow

Example: The weather forecast predicted scattered showers throughout the day, so I carried an umbrella with me.

side /saɪd/

a line forming part of the perimeter of a plane figure

Example: She measured the length of each side of the rectangle to calculate its total perimeter.

either of two parts into which an object, surface, or area can be divided: the right side and the left side

Example: She stood on the left side of the stage, waiting for her cue to enter.

sign /saɪn/

a gesture, mark, or symbol intended to convey an idea or information

Example: She made a thumbs-up sign to indicate her approval and satisfaction with the outcome.

a board or placard displayed in public and intended to advertise, inform, or warn

Example: The "No Parking" sign clearly indicated that vehicles were not allowed to park in that designated area.

signature /sˈɪgnɪtʃɚ/

a person's name written by himself or herself, used in signing something

Example: He put his signature at the bottom of the contract to indicate his agreement and acceptance of the terms.

a distinctive characteristic that identifies a person or animal

Example: His bright red hair was his signature, making him easily recognizable in a crowd.

significance /sɪgnˈɪfɪkəns/

the effect something is likely to have on other things

Example: The historical event had profound significance, shaping the course of the nation's future.

singer /sˈɪŋɚ/

a person who sings, especially professionally

Example: The singer captivated the audience with her powerful vocals and heartfelt performance.

sir /sˈʌr/

a polite term of address for a man

Example: The customer respectfully addressed the manager as "sir" when seeking assistance with a product.

Sir /sˈʌr/

title placed before the name of a knight or baronet

Example: Sir Isaac Newton, the esteemed physicist, made groundbreaking contributions to the field of science.

sister /sˈɪstɚ/

a woman or girl having the same parents as another person

Example: Sarah is my sister, and we share a close bond as siblings.

a female nurse in charge of a ward

Example: The sister on duty swiftly attended to the patient's needs.

site /sˈaɪt/

the piece of ground where something was, is, or is intended to be located

Example: They visited the historical site where an ancient civilization once thrived.

situation /sˌɪtʃuːˈeɪʃən/

a complex or critical state of affairs

Example: John found himself in a difficult situation after accidentally locking his keys inside the car.

location and surroundings

Example: We chose a restaurant for its prime situation in the heart of the city.

size /sˈaɪz/

the dimensions, amount, or extent of something

Example: The size of the room was small, making it cozy and intimate for gatherings.

skill /skˈɪl/

special ability or expertise enabling one to perform an activity very well

Example: The surgeon's skill and precision in the operating room saved countless lives.

skyscraper /skˈaɪskreɪpɚ/

a very tall building

Example: The city skyline was dominated by towering skyscrapers.

snowboard /snˈoʊbɔːrd/

a shaped board, like a skateboard without wheels, on which a person stands to slide across the snow

Example: The snowboarder gracefully glided down the mountain, effortlessly maneuvering the slopes with skill and precision.

society /səsˈaɪəti/

a group of people forming a single community with its own distinctive culture and institutions

Example: Society has evolved over time, adapting to new social norms and values.

software /sˈɔftwɛr/

the programs used with a computer

Example: The software allowed the graphic designer to create stunning visual effects.

soil /sˈɔɪl/

the top layer of the land surface of the earth

Example: The farmer carefully tilled the soil before planting the seeds.

solution /səlˈuːʃən/

the act or process of solving a problem

Example: The teacher guided the students through the steps of finding a solution to the math equation.

a mixture of two or more substances in which the molecules or atoms of the substances are completely dispersed

Example: The chemist prepared a solution by dissolving salt in water until it completely dispersed.

son /sˈʌn/

a male offspring

Example: The proud father held his newborn son in his arms.

song /sˈɔŋ/

a piece of music with words, composed for the voice

Example: The radio played a catchy pop song that instantly became a hit among listeners.

the tuneful call made by certain birds or insects

Example: The melodious song of the nightingale filled the forest, enchanting all who heard it.

songster /sˈɒŋstɚ/

a person who sings, especially fluently and skillfully

Example: The songster mesmerized the audience with her beautiful melodies.

soprano /səprˈɑːnoʊ/

the highest adult female voice of a singer

Example: Her soprano vocals resonated through the halls of prestigious opera.

sound /sˈaʊnd/

anything that can be heard

Example: The sound of laughter filled the room, indicating that everyone was having a great time.

soup /sˈuːp/

a food made by cooking meat, fish, or vegetables in a stock

Example: The restaurant offered a variety of soups on their menu, including tomato, mushroom, and clam chowder.

source /sˈɔːrs/

the origin or starting point

Example: The river was a source of fresh water for the entire village.

any person, book, or organization that provides information for a news report or for research

Example: The researcher cited a reputable academic source in their study to support their hypothesis.

space /spˈeɪs/

a blank portion or area

Example: The artist left an unpainted space on the canvas, allowing the viewer to interpret its meaning.

the unlimited three-dimensional expanse in which all objects exist

Example: The astronauts marveled at the vastness of space as they floated outside the spacecraft.

spacecraft /spˈeɪskræft/

a vehicle that can be used for travel in space

Example: The spacecraft launched into orbit, carrying a crew of astronauts on a mission to the International Space Station.

speaker /spˈiːkɚ/

a person who speaks, especially making a speech

Example: The keynote speaker delivered an inspiring speech at the conference.

Speaker /spˈiːkɚ/

the official chairman of law-making body

Example: The Speaker of the House called the legislative session to order and facilitated the proceedings.

species /spˈiːʃiːz/

one of the groups into which a genus is divided, the members of which are able to interbreed

Example: There are over 1,000 known species of birds, each with unique characteristics and habitats.

speech /spˈiːtʃ/

the ability to speak

Example: The toddler's speech development is progressing rapidly.

a talk given to an audience

Example: His speech at the conference was captivating and well-delivered.

speed /spˈiːd/

the rate at which something moves or happens

Example: The car accelerated to a high speed on the highway.

sport /spˈoːrt/

an activity for exercise, pleasure, or competition

Example: She enjoys playing cricket as a sport to stay active and have fun.

square /skwˈɛr/

a geometric figure with four equal sides and four right angles

Example: She cut out a square piece of fabric to use for her sewing project.

the number produced when a number is multiplied by itself

Example: The square of 5 is 25.

stack /stɑk/

a pile of things, one on top of the other

Example: The stack of documents on his desk seemed never-ending.

staff /stˈæf/

the people employed in a company, school, or organization

Example: The hospital's nursing staff worked tirelessly to provide quality care to patients.

a stick with some special use, such as a walking stick

Example: She used a staff to help her maintain balance.

standard /stˈændɚd/

a level of quality

Example: The hotel's amenities and services were of a superior standard compared to others in the area.

an accepted example of something against which others are judged or measured

Example: The Olympic record set by the athlete became the standard for future competitors.

star /stˈɑːr/

a planet or meteor visible in the clear night sky as a point of light

Example: The North Star guided sailors and explorers in ancient times.

an emblem with five or more radiating points often used as a symbol of rank

Example: The general proudly wore a uniform adorned with a golden star on the shoulder.

state /stˈeɪt/

the condition or circumstances of a person or thing

Example: After the accident, his physical state was critical.

statement /stˈeɪtmənt/

something stated, usually a formal prepared announcement or reply

Example: She issued a statement apologizing for her controversial remarks.

steak /stˈeɪk/

a lean piece of beef for grilling or frying

Example: She seasoned the steak with salt and pepper before placing it on the grill.

a thick slice of pork, veal, or fish

Example: They served a delectable salmon steak, marinated in a tangy citrus glaze.

step /stˈɛp/

the act of moving and setting down one's foot, such as when walking

Example: The soldier's boots echoed with each heavy step as they marched in formation.

a level or stage in a process or sequence of events

Example: The first step in learning to play the piano is to familiarize yourself with the musical notes.

the part of a stair on which one's foot is placed when ascending or descending

Example: She carefully placed her foot on each step of the staircase, descending slowly to avoid tripping.

stereo /stˈɛrɪˌoʊ/

a music system in which sound is directed through speakers

Example: He turned on the stereo and enjoyed the rich, immersive sound coming from the speakers.

steward /stˈuːɚd/

a person who looks after passengers and serves meals on a ship or aircraft

Example: The attentive steward promptly responded to the passenger's request for a blanket and pillow.

a person who administers someone else's property

Example: The estate steward managed the vast property on behalf of the wealthy landowner.

a person who manages the eating arrangements, staff, or service at a club or hotel

Example: As the head steward, he trained and supervised the waitstaff to deliver impeccable service to the club's members.

stewardess /stˈuːɚdˌɛs/

a female steward on an aircraft or ship

Example: The stewardess greeted passengers with a warm smile as they boarded the airplane.

stock /stˈɔːk/

the total amount of goods kept on the premises of a shop or business

Example: The store manager ensured that the stock was replenished regularly to meet customer demands.

the money raised by a company through selling shares entitling their holders to dividends, partial ownership, and usually voting rights

Example: The company issued new shares of stock to raise funds for its expansion plans.

farm animals bred and kept for their meat, skin, etc.

Example: The dairy farm had a healthy stock of cows that provided fresh milk daily.

a liquid produced by simmering meat, fish, or vegetables, and used to make soups and sauces

Example: The homemade stock added depth and richness to the stew.

storage /stˈoːrɪdʒ/

the act of storing or the state of being stored

Example: The storage of hazardous materials requires special precautions and safety measures.

store /stˈoːr/

a large shop

Example: The toy store was filled with shelves of colourful toys and games.

story /stˈoːri/

a description of a chain of events told or written in prose or verse

Example: She wrote a short story about a young detective solving a mysterious crime.

stranger /strˈeɪndʒɚ/

any person whom one does not know

Example: A stranger approached me on the street and asked for directions.

strategy /strˈætədʒi/

a long-term plan for success, such as in politics or business

Example: The company developed a new marketing strategy to increase its market share.

strength /strˈɛŋth/

the state or quality of being physically or mentally strong

Example: His strength allowed him to lift heavy weights effortlessly at the gym.

something regarded as valuable or a source of power

Example: His ability to remain calm and composed under pressure was his greatest strength as a leader.

potency or effectiveness, such as of a drug

Example: The cough syrup had a low strength, so the pharmacist recommended taking it multiple times a day.

stress /strˈɛs/

mental, emotional, or physical strain or tension

Example: The demanding job and long working hours led to high levels of stress for the employees.

special emphasis or significance

Example: The stress placed on punctuality in our workplace is crucial for maintaining efficiency.

strictness /strˈɪktnəs/

the quality or condition of being strict

Example: The strictness of the judge resulted in harsh penalties for the convicted criminals.

structure /strˈʌktʃɚ/

the way the individual parts of something are made, built, or organized into a whole

Example: The structure was damaged by fire.

the pattern of interrelationships within an organization, society, etc.

Example: We need to improve the overall structure of our committee.

student /stˈuːdənt/

a person following a course of study in a school, college, or university

Example: The student raised her hand to ask a question during the lecture.

studio /stˈuːdɪˌoʊ/

a room in which an artist, photographer, or musician works

Example: The photographer transformed the empty studio into a professional photo shoot set.

study /stˈʌdi/

the act or process of studying

Example: I need to find a quiet place for my study.

a room used for studying, reading, or writing

Example: The study had large windows that let in plenty of natural light.

style /stˈaɪl/

form of appearance, design, or production

Example: Her thick black hair had just been styled before the interview.

the way in which something is done

Example: She has not lost her grace and style.

subject /sˈʌbd͡ʒɛkt/

the person, thing, or topic being dealt with or discussed

Example: The subject of today's meeting is the new marketing strategy for our product launch.

a word or phrase that represents the person or thing performing the action of the verb in a sentence

Example: In the sentence "The dog barked loudly," "dog" is the subject.

success /səksˈɛs/

the achievement of something attempted

Example: The entrepreneur's business venture turned out to be a huge success.

succubus /sˈʌkjuːbəs/

female demon fabled to have sex with sleeping men

Example: The protagonist in the horror novel encountered a succubus in his dreams, which added an eerie element to the storyline.

suggestion /səd͡ʒˈɛstʃən/

a hint or indication

Example: I received a great suggestion from a friend on how to organize my workspace for better productivity.

sun /sˈʌn/

the star that is the source of heat and light for the planets in the solar system

Example: The sun rose early, painting the sky with hues of orange and pink, signaling the start of a new day.

sunshine /sˈʌnʃaɪn/

the light and warmth from the sun

Example: The children ran outside to bask in the sunshine, enjoying the warmth on their faces.

supermarket /sˈuːpɚmˌɑːrkɪt/

a large self-service shop selling food and household goods

Example: The supermarket had a wide range of options, from organic and gluten-free products to international cuisine ingredients.

surgery /sˈʌːdʒɚri/

medical treatment in which a person's body is cut open by a surgeon to treat or remove the problem part

Example: The team of doctors conducted a delicate brain surgery to remove a tumour and relieve pressure on the patient's brain.

swarm /swˈɔːrm/

a large or dense group of flying insects

Example: As the sun began to set, a swarm of fireflies illuminated the night sky with their gentle flickering lights.

swine /swˈaɪn/

a mammal with a long head, a snout, and bristle-covered skin, which is kept and killed for pork, ham, and bacon

Example: The farmer raised a herd of swine on his farm.

a mean or unpleasant person

Example: He behaves like a swine, thinking he is better than everyone else.

sympathy /sˈɪmpəθi/

understanding of other people's problems

Example: The counsellor showed great sympathy towards the grieving family, offering them comfort and understanding during their time of loss.

system /sˈɪstəm/

a method or set of methods for doing or organizing something

Example*:*   The healthcare facility introduced an efficient system for patient scheduling.

an ordered manner

Example*:*   My morning routine is a system that helps me start the day on a positive note

Tt

table /tˈeɪbəl/

a piece of furniture consisting of a flat top supported by legs

Example: We gathered around the table for a family dinner and shared stories from our day.

tale /tˈeɪl/

to report malicious stories or trivial complaints

Example: He spread false tales about his co-worker to tarnish his reputation.

a report, account, or story

Example: The old man at the park shared a fascinating tale about his adventures as a young sailor.

task /tˈæsk/

a specific piece of work required to be done

Example: My boss gave me a new task today that I need to complete by the end of the week.

tax /tˈɑks/

a compulsory payment to a government to raise revenue, levied on income, property, or goods and services

Example: We received a notice from the tax office stating that our property tax payment is due next month.

tea /tˈiː/

a drink made by infusing the dried chopped leaves of an Asian shrub in boiling water

Example: After a long day at work, I love to relax with a book and a steaming cup of tea.

teacher /tˈiːtʃɚ/

a person whose job is to teach others, especially children

Example: Teachers often go above and beyond to ensure their students receive a quality education.

teacup /tˈiːkʌp/

a cup out of which tea may be drunk

Example: The teacup slipped from my hand and shattered into pieces on the floor.

teapot /tˈiːpɔːt)

a container with a lid, spout, and handle, in which tea is made and from which it is served

Example: My grandmother's silver teapot has been passed down through generations in our family.

teardrop /tˈɪrdrɔːp/

a single tear

Example: A teardrop rolled down her cheek as she listened to the sad news.

technology /tɛknˈɑːlədʒi/

the application of practical or mechanical sciences to industry or commerce

Example: The rapid advancements in technology have revolutionized various industries, such as healthcare and transportation.

teeth /tˈiːθ/

the plural of tooth

Example: My dentist advised me to floss regularly to keep my teeth clean and healthy.

television /tˈɛlɪvˌɪʒən/

the system or process of producing a moving image with accompanying sound on a distant screen

Example: The television in our living room stopped working, so we had to get it repaired.

temperature /tˈɛmprɪtʃɚ/

the hotness or coldness of something, as measured on a scale that has one or more fixed reference points

Example: The temperature outside is quite hot today, so I will be staying indoors.

tempter /tˈɛmptɚ/

a person or thing that tempts

Example: The salesperson at the store was a skilled tempter, enticing customers with irresistible deals.

temptress /tˈɛmptrəs/

a woman who tempts someone to do something, typically a sexually attractive woman who sets out to allure or seduce someone

Example: The temptress used her seductive powers to manipulate others and get what she wanted.

tennis /tˈɛnɪs/

a game played between two players or pairs of players who use a racket to hit a ball to and fro over a net on a rectangular court

Example: She has been practicing tennis for years and has become quite skilled at it.

tension /tˈɛnʃən/

a situation or condition of hostility, suspense, or uneasiness

Example: The tension between the two rival teams was palpable during the championship game.

a force that stretches or the state or degree of being stretched tight

Example: The tension in the rubber band increased as it was stretched further.

term /tˈʌrm/

a word or expression, especially one used in a specialized field of knowledge

Example: He used a legal term that I did not understand, so I asked for clarification.

a period

***Example*:** The school term starts in September and ends in June.

test /tˈɛst/

a method, practice, or examination designed to ascertain a person or thing

***Example*:** The teacher handed out a spelling test to assess our spelling skills.

the hard outer covering of certain invertebrates

***Example*:** The test of a sea urchin provides protection and support for its delicate internal structures.

thanks /θˈɑŋks/

an expression of appreciation or gratitude

***Example*:** Thanks for helping me carry these heavy bags.

theory /θˈiəri/

a set of ideas, based on evidence and careful reasoning, which offers an explanation of how something works or why something happens, but has not been completely proved

***Example*:** She presented a new theory about the origins of the universe during the scientific conference.

thief /θˈiːf/

a person who steals something from another

***Example*:** The thief broke into the house and stole valuable jewelry.

thing /θˈɪŋ/

any physical object that is not alive that cannot or need not be precisely named

***Example*:** I found a shiny thing on the ground and picked it up out of curiosity.

thought /θˈɔːt/

the act or process of thinking

***Example*:** Her thought was interrupted by a loud noise outside the window.

throat /θrˈoʊt/

the passage from the mouth and nose to the stomach and lungs

Example: He felt a tickle in his throat and started coughing.

thunderstorm /θˈʌndɚstˌɔːrm/

a storm with thunder and lightning and usually heavy rain or hail

Example: The thunderstorm knocked out the power in our neighborhood.

tiger /tˈaɪgɚ/

a large Asian mammal of the cat family which has a tawny yellow coat with black stripes

Example: The documentary showcased the hunting techniques of tigers in the wild.

time /tˈaɪm/

the past, present, or future regarded as a continuous whole

Example: The concept of time fascinates me.

timetable /tˈaɪmteɪbəl/

a schedule or plan that outlines the timing and sequence of events, activities, or tasks, especially in relation to transportation, classes, or events

Example: The airline provided us with a detailed timetable of flight departures and arrivals.

tiredness /tˈaɪɚdnəs/

the state of wishing for sleep or rest; weariness

Example: He decided to call it a night and head to bed due to overwhelming tiredness.

tolerance /tˈɔːlɚrəns/

the quality of accepting other people's rights to their own opinions, beliefs, or actions

Example: We should strive for tolerance and acceptance, even when we disagree with someone's beliefs or opinions.

capacity to endure something, especially pain or hardship

Example: Building mental resilience requires developing a higher tolerance for stress and adversity.

tomato /təmɔtoʊ/

a red fleshy juicy fruit with many edible seeds, eaten in salads, as a vegetable, etc.

Example: She grows tomatoes in her backyard garden and often shares them with neighbours.

tongue /t'ʌŋ/

a movable mass of muscular tissue attached to the floor of the mouth, used for tasting, eating, and speaking

Example: I burned my tongue on a hot slice of pizza.

a language, dialect, or idiom

Example: Guyanese Creole English is my mother tongue, but I am also fluent in Spanish.

a flap of leather on a shoe

Example: Make sure the tongue is centred and straight when you tie your shoelaces for a proper fit.

tool /t'u:l/

an implement, such as a hammer, saw, or spade, that is used by hand to help do a particular type of work

Example: Having the right tools makes the job much easier and more efficient.

a person used to perform dishonourable or unpleasant tasks for another

Example: She became a tool for her friends.

tooth /t'u:θ/

one of the bonelike projections in the jaws of most vertebrates that are used for biting, tearing, or chewing

Example: He accidentally bit into something hard and chipped his front tooth.

top /tˈɑːp/

the highest point or part of anything

Example: *The mountaineer reached the top of the mountain after a grueling climb.*

the most important or successful position

Example: *The actor's outstanding performance earned him a spot at the top in the film industry.*

topic /tˈɔːpɪk/

a subject of a speech, book, conversation, etc.

Example: *We had an interesting conversation about the topic of travel destinations.*

town /tˈaʊn/

a large group of houses, shops, factories, etc., smaller than a city and larger than a village

Example: *I live in a small town surrounded by beautiful countryside.*

trade /trˈeɪd/

the buying and selling of goods and services

Example: *International trade plays a vital role in the global economy.*

tradition /trædˈɪʃən/

the handing down from generation to generation of customs, beliefs, etc.

Example: *It is a tradition in our family to gather around the fireplace and share stories during the holidays.*

trainer /trˈeɪnɚ/

a person who coaches a person or team in a sport

Example: *The basketball team hired a new trainer to improve their performance.*

training /trˈeɪnɪŋ/

the process of bringing a person to an agreed standard of proficiency by practice and instructions

Example: The soccer team's coach emphasized the importance of regular training for optimal performance.

traitor /trˈeɪɾɚ/

a person who betrays friends, country, a cause, etc.

Example: The spy was considered a traitor to his own country, having infiltrated sensitive government agencies, and compromised national security.

transportation /trænspoːrtˈeɪʃən/

a means or system of carrying or moving from one place to another

Example: I rely on my car for transportation, especially when I need to travel to areas not easily accessible by public transport.

trend /trˈɛnd/

general tendency or direction

Example: There is a trend towards remote work and flexible schedules in many industries.

fashionable style

Example: Skinny jeans were a major trend a few years ago, but now looser, relaxed-fit jeans are making a comeback.

troupe /trˈuːp/

a company of actors or other performers

Example: The dance troupe dazzled the audience with their synchronized moves and vibrant costumes.

trout /trˈaʊt/

any of various game fishes related to the salmon and found chiefly in fresh water in northern regions

Example: Trout fishing season opens next month, and I cannot wait to head to the lake and try my luck.

truth /trˈuːθ/

the quality of being true, genuine, or factual

Example: Sometimes the truth can be painful, but it is necessary for growth and understanding.

two /t'uː/

the cardinal number that is the sum of one and one

Example: The recipe calls for two cups of flour.

type /t'aɪp/

a kind, class, or category of things, all of which have something in common

Example: My sister loves trying out different types of cuisine, from Italian to Thai to Mexican.

Uu

ulcer /ˈəlsɚ/

an open sore on the surface of the skin or a mucous membrane

Example: My grandmother has been suffering from a chronic leg ulcer that just will not heal.

ulster /ˈəlstɚ/

a man's heavy double-breasted overcoat

Example: When I visited London, I noticed many gentlemen wearing ulster to stay warm in the chilly weather.

ultimatum /ˌəltəˈmeɪtəm/

a final warning to someone that they must agree to certain conditions or requirements, or else action will be taken against them

Example: My roommate gave me an ultimatum: clean up my mess or find a new place to live.

ultra /ˈəltrə/

a person who has extreme or immoderate beliefs or opinions

Example: She's an ultra when it comes to environmental issues and can get quite heated in debates.

ultrasound /ˌəltrəˈsaʊnd/

ultrasonic waves, used in echo sounding, medical diagnosis, and therapy

Example: During the pregnancy, the doctor performed an ultrasound to monitor the growth and development of the baby.

umbrage /ˈəmbrɪdʒ/

to take offence

Example: He took umbrage at her remarks, feeling insulted and hurt by her words.

umbrella /ˈəmˌbrɛlə/

a portable device used for protection against rain, consisting of a light canopy supported on a collapsible metal frame mounted on a central rod

Example:　　She opened her colourful umbrella to shield herself from the heavy rain.

a single organization, idea, etc., that contains or covers many different organizations or ideas

Example:　　The fashion brand operates as an umbrella for several subsidiary companies, each specializing in a specific product line.

umpire /ˈəmˌpaɪɚ/

an official who ensures that the people taking part in a game follow the rules

Example:　　The umpire made a crucial call during the cricket match, determining whether the runner was safe or out.

uncle /ˈʌŋkəl/

a brother of one's father or mother

Example:　　My uncle is a talented musician.

underclass /ˈəndɚˌklæs/

a class beneath the usual social scale consisting of the most disadvantaged people, such as the long-term unemployed

Example:　　The underclass often struggles to break the cycle of poverty and find stable employment.

undercoat /ˈəndɚˌkoʊt/

a coat of paint applied before the top coat

Example:　　Before applying the final colour, make sure to apply a layer of undercoat to ensure a smooth and even finish.

a layer of soft fur beneath the outer fur of animals such as the otter

Example:　　During shedding season, the dog's undercoat tends to come out in clumps, requiring regular grooming to maintain a tidy appearance.

underdog /ˈəndɚˌdɔg/

a person or team in a weak or underprivileged position

Example: The underdog team surprised everyone by defeating the reigning champions in a thrilling match.

understanding /ˌʌndɚˈstændɪŋ/

the ability to learn, judge, or make decisions

Example: The professor's deep understanding of literature allowed him to analyze and interpret classic novels with great insight.

an opinion or interpretation of a subject

Example: Each person's understanding of art is subjective, as it is influenced by their own experiences and perspectives.

a mutual agreement, usually an informal or private one

Example: The two friends had an understanding that they would always support each other through thick and thin.

undertaker /ˈəndɚˌteɪkɚ/

a person whose job is to look after the bodies of people who have died and to organize funerals

Example: The undertaker helped us choose a beautiful casket and arrange the details of the memorial service.

underworld /ˈəndɚˌwɝld/

criminals and their associates

Example: The police are working tirelessly to dismantle the underworld and bring notorious criminals to justice.

unease /əˈniz/

anxiety or nervousness

Example: There was an air of unease in the office after the announcement of upcoming layoffs.

unemployment /ˌənɪmˈplɔɪmənt/

the condition of being unemployed

Example: The recent economic downturn has led to a significant increase in unemployment.

unicycle /ˈjunəˌsaɪkəl/

a one-wheeled vehicle driven by pedals, used in circus

Example: My friend is an expert at riding a unicycle.

uniform /ˈjunəˌfɔrm/

a special identifying set of clothes for the members of an organization, such as soldiers

Example: The students wore their school uniform, consisting of a white shirt and navy-blue pants or skirt.

union /ˈjuːniən/

the act of merging two or more things to become one

Example: The union of the two companies resulted in a stronger market presence and increased profitability.

marriage

Example: We celebrated the union of Ava and Jack all night.

unionism /ˈjunjəˌnɪzəm/

adherence to the principles of trade unions

Example: Unionism plays a vital role in protecting the rights and interests of workers in various industries.

unison /ˈjunəsən/

at the same time as another person or other people

Example: The dancers moved in perfect unison with each other.

unit /ˈjuːnɪt/

a single undivided entity or whole

Example: The apartment complex consists of several units, each equipped with its own kitchen and bathroom.

the digit or position immediately to the left of the decimal point

Example: In the number 3.14, the 3 is in the unit's place, representing three whole units.

universe /ˈjunəˌvɜ˞s/

the whole of all existing matter, energy, and space

Example: The universe is an incredible expanse of galaxies, stars, and planets that continues to fascinate scientists and astronomers.

university /ˌjuːnɪvˈɜːsɪti/

an institution of higher education with authority to award degrees

Example: She studied biology at the university and earned her bachelor's degree.

unreality /ʌnrɪˈælɪti/

the quality of being imaginary, illusory, or unrealistic

Example: Sometimes, when I am immersed in a good book, I find solace in the unreality of the fictional world.

unrest /ənˈrɛst/

a rebellious state of discontent

Example: The police were called to the neighborhood to restore order and calm the growing unrest among the residents.

untruth /ənˈtruθ/

a statement that is not true

Example: He admitted to spreading untruths about his opponent during the election campaign.

unveiling /ənˈveɪlɪŋ/

a ceremony involving the removal of a veil covering a statue

Example: The unveiling of the statue was a beautiful ceremony.

upbringing /ˈəpˌbrɪŋɪŋ/

the education of a person during his or her formative years

Example: Despite facing challenges in his upbringing, he managed to overcome adversity and achieve success.

upheaval /əpˈhivəl/

a strong, sudden, or violent disturbance

Example: The political upheaval in the country resulted in widespread protests.

upholstery /əˈpoʊlstɚi/

the padding, springs, and covering of a chair or sofa

Example: The upholstery of the antique armchair was made from high-quality velvet.

upkeep /ˈəpˌkip/

the act or process of keeping something in good repair

Example: Regular maintenance is crucial for the upkeep of your car, ensuring its longevity and optimal performance.

uprising /ˈəˌpraɪzɪŋ/

a revolt or rebellion

Example: The history books are filled with stories of uprisings by oppressed populations fighting for their rights and freedom.

uproar /ˈəˌprɔr/

a commotion or disturbance characterized by loud noise and confusion

Example: There was an uproar in the classroom when the students discovered that their homework had been eaten by the teacher's dog.

upshot /ˈəpˌʃɒt/

the final result or conclusion

Example: The upshot of the investigation was the identification of the culprit responsible for the data breach.

upstart /ˈəpˌstɑrt/

a person who has risen suddenly to a position of power and behaves arrogantly

Example: The new CEO is quite the upstart, acting like she knows everything and disregarding the expertise of the existing team.

upsurge /ˈəpˌsɜ-dʒ/

a rapid rise or swell

Example: There has been an upsurge in online shopping during the pandemic as more people opt for convenient and contactless shopping experiences.

upswing /ˈəpˌswɪŋ/

any increase or improvement

Example: There has been an upswing in tourism in the region due to the opening of new attractions.

upturn /ˈəpˌtɜ-n/

an upward trend or movement

Example: After a period of economic decline, the country's economy finally showed an upturn with increased GDP growth.

urea /jɚˈiə/

a white soluble crystalline compound found in urine

Example: The laboratory test revealed elevated levels of urea in the patient's urine, indicating potential kidney dysfunction.

urethra /jɚˈiθrə/

the tube that mammals carry urine from the bladder out of the body

Example: The doctor explained that a blockage in the urethra was causing difficulty in urination.

urge /ˈɜ-dʒ/

a strong impulse, inner drive, or yearning

Example: The urge to help others led her to volunteer at the local homeless shelter.

urology /jɚˈɑlədʒi/

the branch of medicine concerned with the urinary system and its diseases

Example: The urology department at the hospital offers comprehensive care for patients with urinary tract infections.

user /jˈuːzɚ/

a person who uses or operates something

Example: Anna is a regular user of social media platforms like Facebook and Instagram.

usher /ˈəʃɚ/

an official who shows people to their seats

Example: The usher at the concert hall was very helpful.

utensil /juˈtɛnsəl/

a tool or container for practical use

Example: When camping, it is essential to bring lightweight and versatile utensils for cooking and eating.

uterus /ˈjutɚəs/

a hollow muscular organ in the pelvic cavity of female mammals, which houses the developing fetus

Example: My sister is pregnant, and her doctor said that the baby is healthy and developing well in her uterus.

utterance /ˈətɚəns/

something expressed in speech or writing

Example: During the argument, her hurtful utterance left him feeling deeply wounded and upset.

vacancy /ˈveɪkənsi/

an unoccupied job or position

Example: Peter's retirement has created a vacancy for the role of sales manager.

vacation /veɪˈkeɪʃən/

a period in which a break is taken from work or studies for rest or recreation

Example: We decided to go on a camping vacation to enjoy nature and disconnect from technology.

vaccine /ˌvækˈsin/

a substance made from the germs that cause a disease which is given to people to prevent them getting the disease

Example: The doctor advised me to get a tetanus vaccine after I stepped on a rusty nail.

vacuum /ˈvækjum/

a space which contains no air or other gas

Example: The scientist conducted experiments in a vacuum chamber to study the behaviour of certain materials in the absence of air.

vagabond /ˈvæɡəbɑnd/

a person who travels from place to place and has no fixed home or job

Example: The local shelter provides support and resources for vagabonds, offering them a temporary place to stay and access to job opportunities.

vagary /ˈveɪɡɚi/

an unpredictable change in a situation or in someone's behaviour

Example: The sudden decision to quit his job was just another one of his vagaries.

vagrant /ˈveɪgrənt/

a person who moves from place to place and has no regular home or job

Example: The city's social services department provides support and resources for vagrants to help them find stable housing.

valence /ˈveɪləns/

the ability of atoms and chemical groups to form compounds

Example: The chemist analyzed the valence of the molecule to determine its reactivity and potential bonding patterns.

valentine /ˈvælənˌtaɪn/

a person to whom a card is sent as an expression of love on Saint Valentine's Day, February 14

Example: My best friend holds a special place in my heart and is my valentine.

valet /væˈleɪ/

a male servant employed to look after another man

Example: The wealthy businessman arrived at the event accompanied by his valet, who ensured he looked impeccable.

Valium /ˈveɪliəm/

a drug used as a tranquilizer

Example: The doctor prescribed Valium for her anxiety.

valley /ˈvæli/

a long stretch of land between hills, often with a river flowing through it

Example: The valley is home to many farms and orchards, making it a fertile and productive agricultural region.

valour /ˈvælɚ/

great bravery

Example: The soldier showed great valour on the battlefield, risking his life to protect his comrades.

valuation /vælju'eɪʃən/

a formal assessment of how much something is worth

Example: The real estate agent conducted a valuation of the property to provide an estimate of its value for potential buyers.

value /v'ælju:/

the desirability of something, often in terms of its usefulness or exchangeability

Example: When buying a smartphone, I always consider the value it offers in terms of its features and performance.

an amount of money considered to be a fair exchange for something

Example: The car's resale value dropped significantly after the accident.

valve /'vɔlv/

a part attached to a pipe or tube which controls the flow of gas or liquid

Example: To drain the pool, we had to open the valve at the bottom and let the water out.

a small flap in a hollow organ, such as the heart, that controls the flow and direction of blood

Example: The doctor discovered a faulty valve in my heart, which was causing irregular blood flow.

vampire /'vɑmpaɪr/

a corpse that rises nightly from its grave to drink the blood of living people

Example: The TV show we watched last night had an intriguing storyline about a group of vampires living among humans, struggling to keep their supernatural identity a secret.

van /'vɑn/

a four-wheeler road vehicle, with a roof and no side windows, used to transport goods

Example: The local bakery uses a van to deliver freshly baked goods to various shops and cafes in the area.

vandal /ˈvɑndəl/

someone who deliberately causes damage to personal or public property

Example: The authorities are working hard to identify and apprehend the vandals responsible for the destruction of public property.

vane /ˈveɪn/

one of the blades forming part of the wheel of a windmill, a screw propeller, etc.

Example: The vane on top of the windmill turned with the wind, indicating the direction and strength of the breeze.

vanguard /ˈvɑn‚gɑrd/

a group of people leading the way in new developments or ideas

Example: The vanguard of medical researchers is dedicated to finding innovative treatments and cures for previously incurable diseases.

vanity /ˈvɑnəti/

a feeling of pride about one's appearance or ability

Example: His vanity was evident as he constantly boasted about his achievements and sought validation from others.

vantage /ˈvɑntədʒ/

a state, position, or opportunity offering advantage

Example: The team's early lead provided them with a vantage, giving them a better chance of winning the game.

vapour /ˈveɪpɚ/

a mass of tiny drops of water or other liquids in the air, which appear as a mist

Example: The hot shower created a cloud of vapour in the bathroom, making it feel like a steam room.

variance /ˈvɛriəns/

not in agreement

Example: There was a significant variance between the budgeted and actual expenses, leading to a financial shortfall.

variation /vˌɛrɪˈeɪʃən/

something presented in a slightly different form

Example: The recipe allows for variations, so you can add different vegetables or spices to suit your taste.

variety /vɚˈaɪəti/

different things of the same kind

Example: The bookstore has a great variety of genres, catering to different reading preferences.

varnish /ˈvɑrnɪʃ/

a liquid painted onto a surface to give it a hard glossy finish

Example: The carpenter meticulously applied varnish to the handmade furniture, ensuring a smooth and durable finish.

an artificial, superficial, or deceptively pleasing manner or appearance

Example: The extravagant lifestyle she portrayed on social media had a varnish of glamour, hiding the financial struggles she faced.

vas deferens /vˈæs dˈɛfrənz/

either of the two ducts that convey sperm from the testicles to the penis

Example: The doctor explained that the vas deferens carries mature sperm from the epididymis to the ejaculatory ducts.

vase /ˈvɑz/

a glass or pottery jar used as an ornament or for holding flowers

Example: The florist recommended using a tall, cylindrical vase for the sunflowers I purchased.

vasectomy /væˈsɛktəmi/

surgical removal of all or part of the vas deferens as a method of contraception

Example: Some men opt for a vasectomy as a responsible choice when they feel their family is complete and they no longer desire to have children.

vaudeville /ˈvɔdəvɪl/

variety entertainment consisting of short acts such as song-and-dance routines and comic turns

Example: The theatre downtown used to host vaudeville shows every weekend, where talented performers would showcase their skills to a live audience.

vault /ˈvɔlt/

a secure room where money and other valuables are stored safely

Example: The bank has a highly secure vault where customers' safety deposit boxes are stored, ensuring the protection of their valuable possessions.

vegan /ˈvɛgən/

a person who does not eat meat, fish, or any animal products such as cheese, butter, etc.

Example: My friend became a vegan last year and has since adopted a plant-based diet, avoiding all animal products.

vegetable /ˈvɛdʒtəbəl/

a plant with parts that are used as food

Example: I love to eat a variety of vegetables, such as broccoli, carrots, and spinach, to ensure I get a balanced and nutritious diet.

vegetarian /ˌvɛdʒəˈtɛˌriən/

a person who does not eat meat or fish

Example: My sister recently became a vegetarian after learning about the environmental impact of meat production.

vehicle /vˈiəkəl/

a machine such as a car or a bus for transporting people or goods

Example: The delivery company uses large vehicles to transport goods efficiently and ensure timely deliveries.

something used to achieve a particular purpose or as a means of expression

Example: Music has always been a vehicle for self-expression and a way to connect with others on a deep level.

veil /ˈveɪl/

a piece of thin cloth used to cover a woman's face

Example: The bride wore a beautiful lace veil that cascaded down her back, adding an elegant touch to her wedding attire.

vein /ˈveɪn/

any of the tubes that carry blood to the heart

Example: She had an IV line inserted into a vein in her arm to receive medication and fluids.

vendetta /vɛnˈdɛtə/

a long-lasting quarrel between people or organizations in which they attempt to harm each other

Example: The political rivals engaged in a bitter vendetta, constantly trying to discredit each other and gain the upper hand.

vendor /ˈvɛndɚ/

a person who sells goods such as newspapers from a stall or cart

Example: The local farmers' market is a great place to support local vendors and buy fresh produce.

venom /ˈvɛnəm/

a feeling of great bitterness or anger towards someone

Example: The venom in their family feud had escalated to the point where they no longer spoke to each other.

the poison that certain snakes and scorpions inject when they bite or sting

Example: The medical team administered antivenom to counteract the effects of the snake's venom.

vent /ˈvɛnt/

a small opening in something through which fresh air can enter and fumes can be released

Example: The kitchen has a vent above the stove to remove cooking odours and smoke.

verisimilitude /ˌvɛrəsəˈmɪləˌtud/

the appearance of truth or reality

Example: The virtual reality game provided an incredible sense of verisimilitude, transporting players into a lifelike environment where they could interact with virtual characters and objects.

version /vˈɜːʒən/

a form of something with some differences from other forms

Example: I am planning to release a new version of my software next month.

vertebrate /ˈvɜtəˌbreɪt/

an animal with a backbone

Example: I went to the zoo yesterday and saw some amazing vertebrates, including lions, giraffes, and penguins.

vertex /vˈɜːtɛks/

the highest point

Example: The mountain peak stood as the vertex of the landscape, offering breath-taking views of the surrounding valleys.

the point on a geometric figure where the sides form an angle

Example: In the geometry class, the students learned how to identify and label the vertex of different polygons.

veto /vˈiːtoʊ/

the power to prevent legislation or action proposed by others

Example: The committee chair has the authority to cast a veto if they believe a decision is not in the best interest of the organization.

victory /vˈɪktəri/

success attained in a contest or struggle

Example: After months of training and preparation, she finally achieved a well-deserved victory in the marathon.

video /vˈɪdioʊ/

the recording and showing of films and events using a television set, video tapes, and a video recorder

Example: The school organized a video presentation to highlight the achievements of the graduating class.

view /vjˈuː/

opinion, judgment, or belief

Example: The teacher encouraged students to express their views during the classroom debate.

village /vˈɪlɪdʒ/

a small group of houses in a country area

Example: There's a charming little village nearby that has a cosy café and an enchanting bookstore.

virtue /ˈvɜtʃu/

a positive moral quality

Example: Perseverance is a virtue that enables us to overcome obstacles and achieve our goals.

virus /vˈaɪrəs/

a microorganism that is smaller than a bacterium and can cause disease in humans, animals, or plants

Example: I caught a virus and have been feeling under the weather for the past few days.

a type of malicious software or malware that infects computer systems and can cause various detrimental effects.

Example: The IT department detected a virus on the company's network and immediately took steps to isolate and remove it.

viscount /vˈaɪkaʊnt/

a nobleman ranking below an earl and above a baron

Example: The viscount inherited the title and estate from his father, continuing the family's long-standing noble lineage.

voice /vˈɔɪs/

the sound made by the vibration of the vocal cords

Example: His voice was so soothing and comforting that it immediately put me at ease.

a category of the verb that expresses whether it is active or passive

Example: The teacher asked the students to identify whether the sentence was in the active or passive voice.

volcano /vɔːlkˈeɪnoʊ/

an opening in the earth's crust from which molten lava, ashes, dust, and gases are ejected from below the earth's surface

Example: We visited Hawaii and witnessed the awe-inspiring power of a volcano erupting.

volition /voʊˈlɪʃən/

the ability to decide things for oneself

Example: He made the decision to quit the job of his own volition, as he felt it was time for a change.

volume /vˈɔːljuːm/

the magnitude of the three-dimensional space enclosed within or occupied by something

Example: The volume of the suitcase exceeded the airline's baggage restrictions.

volunteer / ˌvɔlənˈtɪr/

a person who freely undertakes a task

***Example**:*   *He decided to become a volunteer at the hospital to give back to the community.*

Ww

wad /ˈwɑd/
a small mass of soft material, such as cotton wool, used for packing or stuffing
Example: The tailor used a wad of fabric scraps to stuff the armholes of the dress, creating a better fit.

waders /ˈweɪdɚz/
a long waterproof boot which completely cover the leg
Example: The workers wore waders to protect themselves from the water while cleaning the flooded basement.

wafer /ˈweɪfɚ/
a thin crisp sweetened biscuit
Example: She gave me a wafer as a treat and it satisfied my sweet tooth.

waffle /ˈwɑfəl/
a square crisp pancake with a grid like pattern
Example: I had a delicious waffle with maple syrup and fresh berries for breakfast.

wager /ˈweɪdʒɚ/
a bet on the outcome of an event or activity
Example: The two friends had a wager on who could eat the most chilli peppers in five minutes.

waif /ˈweɪf/
a person, especially a child, who is, or who looks as if he or she might be homeless
Example: The novel tells the heart-warming story of a waif who finds a loving home.

waist /ˈweɪst/
the narrow part of the body between the ribs and the hips

Example: The tailor took her waist measurement to ensure the perfect fit for her new trousers.

waiter /ˈweɪtɚ/

a man who serves people with food and drink in a restaurant

Example: The waiter provided excellent service, ensuring our glasses were always filled.

waitress /ˈweɪtrəs/

a woman who serves people with food and drink in a restaurant

Example: The waitress took our orders and made sure to note any special dietary requests.

waiver /ˈweɪvɚ/

the act or an instance of voluntary giving up a claim or right

Example: The employee signed a waiver agreeing not to hold the company responsible for any accidents.

walkway /ˈwɔˌkweɪ/

a path designed for use by pedestrians

Example: The Park has a beautiful walkway lined with trees, perfect for leisurely strolls.

wallet /ˈwɔlət/

a small folding case for holding paper money and credit cards

Example: His wallet was stolen while he was traveling, causing him a lot of inconvenience.

war /wˈɔːr/

open armed conflict between two or more countries or groups

Example: War brings about immense human suffering and loss, affecting both soldiers and civilians.

wariness /wˈɛrinəs/

caution about possible dangers or problems

Example: The hikers felt a sense of wariness as they entered the dense forest, aware of the wildlife that could be present.

warmth /wˈɔːrmθ/

the state of being warm

Example: The crackling fireplace provided a comforting warmth on a cold winter evening.

affection or cordiality

Example: The hostess welcomed her guests with genuine warmth, ensuring everyone felt comfortable and included.

warning /wˈɔːrnɪŋ/

a hint, threat, or advance notice of a possible danger or problem

Example: The flashing red lights on the dashboard served as a warning that the car's engine was overheating.

water /wˈɔːtɚ/

a clear colourless tasteless liquid that is essential for plant and animal life, that falls as rain, and forms seas, rivers, and lakes

Example: The heavy rain caused the water levels in the river to rise significantly.

way /wˈeɪ/

a manner, method, or means

Example: She found a creative way to solve the problem and impressed everyone with her ingenuity.

weakness /wˈiːknəs/

the state of being weak

Example: His physical weakness prevented him from participating in certain sports activities.

wealth /wˈɛlθ/

a large amount of money and valuable material possessions

Example: Wealth can provide financial security and open opportunities.

weather /wˈɛðɚ/

the day-to-day atmospheric conditions, such as temperature, cloudiness, and rainfall, affecting a specific place

Example: The weather today is sunny and warm, perfect for a picnic in the park.

web /wˈɛb/

a mesh of fine tough threads built by a spider to trap insects

Example: The spider skillfully spun its web between two branches, waiting for its prey.

anything that is intricately formed or complex

Example: The artist created a web of intricate brushstrokes, resulting in a mesmerizing painting.

wedding /wˈɛdɪŋ/

a marriage ceremony

Example: The wedding reception was filled with laughter, dancing, and heartfelt speeches.

week /wˈiːk/

a period of seven consecutive days from a specified day

Example: I will be on vacation for one week, so I won't be available for meetings.

while /wˈaɪl/

a period of time

Example: We chatted for a while before the meeting started.

wife /wˈaɪf/

the woman to whom a man is married

Example: My wife and I have been happily married for over 20 years.

wind /wˈɪnd/

a current of air moving across the earth's surface

Example: The wind blew gently, rustling the leaves on the trees.

gas in the stomach or intestines

Example: I try to avoid eating foods that cause me to have excessive wind, as it can be uncomfortable.

winner /wˈɪnɚ/

a person or thing that wins

Example: The marathon winner crossed the finish line with a huge smile of triumph on her face.

witch /wˈɪt͡ʃ/

a person who practices magic or sorcery, especially black magic

Example: The witch in the fairy tale had a cauldron where she brewed potions and cast spells.

wizard /wˈɪzɚd/

a man in fairy tales who has magical powers

Example: In the movie, the wizard used his powers to help the heroes defeat the evil sorcerer.

a person who is outstandingly gifted in some specified field

Example: James, a coding wizard, can write intricate programs and develop software with ease.

wolf /wˈʊlf/

a predatory doglike wild animal which hunts in packs

Example: During our hike, we spotted a wolf in the distance, gracefully moving through the forest.

woman /wˈʊmən/

an adult female human being with qualities associated with the female, such as tenderness

Example: The woman sitting next to me on the bus offered to help carry my groceries.

women /wˈɪmɪn/

the plural of woman

Example: My mother and sister are incredible women who have always supported and inspired me.

wood /wˈʊd/

the hard fibrous substance beneath the bark in trees and shrubs, which is used in building and carpentry and as fuel

Example: The carpenter used high-quality wood to construct the dining table.

word /wˈʌːd/

the smallest single meaningful unit of speech or writing

Example: The word 'serendipity' has a beautiful sound to it, don't you think?

work /wˈɜːk/

physical or mental effort directed to doing or making something

Example: She's been putting in a lot of work to improve her painting skills.

paid employment at a job, trade, or profession

Example: She is looking for work in the tech industry after completing her computer science degree.

worker /wˈɜːkɚ/

a person who works at a specified job; an employee

Example: I am looking for a reliable worker to help me with the construction project.

world /wˈɜːld/

the earth, together with all of its countries and people

Example: The world is facing many challenges, such as climate change and poverty.

writer /rˈaɪtɚ/

a person whose job is writing

Example: As a writer, she spends most of her day at the computer, typing away at her latest project.

writing /rˈaɪtɪŋ/

something that has been written

Example: Her writing is very clear and concise, which makes it easy to understand and follow.

Xx

x-axis /ˈɛks-ˈæksɪs/

a reference axis, usually horizontal, of a graph along which the x-coordinate is measured

Example: *Yesterday in Mathematics class I learnt that the x-axis represents the range of values for the independent variable, such as time or distance.*

X-chromosome /ˈɛks-krˈoʊməsˌoʊm/

the sex chromosome that occurs in pairs in the females of many animals, including humans, and as one of a pair with the Y-chromosome in males

Example: *The X-chromosome carries many genes that are important for development and functioning of the body.*

xenon /zˈɛnɔːn/

a colourless odourless gas found in minute quantities in the air

Example: *The discovery of xenon was a significant milestone in the history of chemistry and led to a better understanding of the nature of gasses.*

xenophobia /zˌɛnoʊfˈoʊbiə/

hatred or fear of foreigners or strangers

Example: *We need to educate ourselves and others about the harmful effects of xenophobia, and work to build more inclusive and diverse societies.*

xerophyte /zˈiərəfˌaɪt/

a plant such as a cactus, which is adapted for growing or living in dry surroundings

Example: *I just got back from the desert and saw so many interesting xerophytes, like the Joshua tree and the Barrel cactus.*

Xerox /zˈiərɔːks/

a machine for copying printed materials

Example: The office just got a new Xerox machine; it's printing so much faster than the old one.

Xhosa /kˈɔːsə/

an ethnic group in South Africa who predominantly reside in the Eastern Cape province

Example: The Xhosa people have a rich cultural heritage that includes traditional music, dance, and dress.

a Bantu language spoken by the Xhosa people

Example: Xhosa is one of the eleven official languages of South Africa and is spoken by millions of people.

x-ray /ˈɛks-rˈeɪ/

a stream of electromagnetic radiation of a short wavelength that can pass through some solid materials

Example: The doctors ordered an x-ray of a broken bone to determine the extent of the injury and the best course of treatment.

xylem /zˈaɪləm/

a plant tissue that conducts water and mineral salts from the roots to all other parts

Example: The xylem tissue in plants plays an important role in transporting water and nutrients throughout the plant.

xylene /zˈaɪliːn/

a hydrocarbon existing in three isomeric forms, all three being colourless flammable volatile liquids used as solvents and in the manufacture of synthetic resins, dyes, and insecticides

Example: The chemical plant had to take extra safety precautions when working with xylene due to its flammability.

xylophone /zˈaɪləfˌoʊn/

a percussion instrument consisting of a set of wooden bars played with hammers

Example: The band's percussionist played a beautiful solo on the xylophone during the concert.

Yy

yabby /jˈæbi/

a small freshwater crayfish

Example: We caught some yabby in the freshwater stream last weekend and cooked them for dinner.

yacht /jˈɔːt/

a large boat with sails or an engine, used for racing or pleasure cruising

Example: The millionaire businessman arrived at the marina in his luxurious yacht.

yahoo /jˈæhuː/

a crude, brutish, or obscenely coarse person

Example: I was embarrassed by my friend's behaviour when he acted like a yahoo in front of my family.

a multinational technology company that provides internet-related products and services, such as search engines, email, and online advertising.

Example: Rick just received an email from Yahoo about his account being hacked.

yak /jˈæk/

Tibetan ox with long shaggy hair

Example: We saw a herd of yaks grazing on the hills during our trek in the Himalayas.

yam /jˈɑm/

a twining plant of tropical and subtropical regions, cultivated for its starchy roots which are eaten as a vegetable

Example: My dad makes the best yam soup; it is so delicious.

Yankee /jˈɑŋkiː/

a person from the Northern United States

Example: My great-grandfather was a Yankee who fought in the Civil War.

yard /jˈɑːrd/

a unit of length equal to 3 feet (0.9144 metres)

Example: The football field is 100 yards long.

a piece of enclosed or open area, often adjoining or surrounded by a building or buildings

Example: The children are playing in the yard.

yardarm /jˈɑːrdɑːrm/

the outer end of a ship's yard

Example: Marcus was tried and executed by hanging from the fore yardarm.

yardstick /jˈɑːrdstɪk/

a measure or standard used for comparison

Example: The company uses sales figures as a yardstick to measure performance.

a graduated measuring stick one yard long

Example: The tailor used a yardstick to measure the length of the jacket.

yarmulke /jˈɑːrmʌlk/

a skullcap worn by Jewish men

Example: The bar mitzvah boy wore a yarmulke embroidered with his name and the date of his ceremony.

yarn /jˈɑːrn/

a continuous twisted strand of natural or synthetic fibres, used for knitting or making cloth

Example: This sweater is made of cotton yarns.

yarrow /jˈæroʊ/

a wild plant with flat clusters of white flowers

Example: Yarrow can often be found growing in gardens during the summer months.

yashmak /jˈæʃmæk/

a veil worn by a Muslim woman to cover her face in public

Example: In some countries, the wearing of a yashmak is mandatory for women in public spaces.

yawl /Jˈɔːl/

a two-masted sailing boat

Example: The crew of the yawl had to navigate through stormy and rough seas to reach the port.

yaws /jˈɔːs/

an infectious disease of tropical climates characterized by red skin eruptions

Example: Anjie contracted yaws while on a trip to a tropical country and she had to be treated with antibiotics.

Y-chromosome /wˈaɪ-krˈoʊməsˌoʊm/

the sex chromosome that occurs as one pair with the X-chromosome in the males of many mammals, including humans

Example: The doctor ordered a genetic test to check for any abnormalities in the patient's Y-chromosome.

year /jˈɪr/

a period of twelve months from any specified date

Example: I am planning to take a year off from work to travel the world.

yearbook /jˈɪrbʊk/

a reference book published once a year containing details of events of the previous year

Example: I love looking through my old high school yearbooks and reminiscing about the good times.

yearling /jˈɪrlɪŋ/

an animal that is between one and two years old

Example: The farmer had to separate the yearling calves from the older cows to avoid overcrowding in the pasture.

yeast /jˈiːst/

a yellowish fungus used in fermenting alcoholic drinks and in raising dough for bread

Example: I need to buy some yeast for the bread recipe I am making tonight.

yellow /jˈɛloʊ/

the colour of an egg yolk

Example: The sunflowers in the field were a bright shade of yellow.

yellow fever /jˈɛloʊ fˈiːvɚ/

an acute infectious tropical disease-causing fever and jaundice, caused by certain mosquitoes

Example: My friend got sick with yellow fever when she went on a backpacking trip in South America.

yellowhammer /jˈɛloʊhˌæmɚ/

a European songbird with a yellowish head and body

Example: I heard a yellowhammer singing outside my window this morning.

Yen /jˈɛn/

the standard monetary unit of Japan

Example: The Yen has been the official currency of Japan since 1871.

yeoman /jˈoʊmən/

a farmer owning and farming his own land

Example: My great-grandfather was a yeoman who owned a small farm in the countryside.

yesterday /jˈɛstɚdˌeɪ/

the day before today

Example: Yesterday was a busy day at work, I had back-to-back meetings all day long.

yew /jˈuː/

an evergreen tree with needle-like leaves, red berries, and fine-grained elastic wood

Example: The yew tree in my backyard has been there for over 50 years and is still going strong.

yoga /jˈoʊgə/

a Hindu system of philosophy aiming at spiritual, mental, and physical well-being by means of deep meditation, prescribed postures, and controlled breathing

Example: Yoga has helped me manage my stress and anxiety by allowing me to do breathing techniques and mindfulness.

yogi /jˈoʊgi/

a person who practices or is a master of yoga

Example: The famous yogi demonstrated some advanced yoga poses that I had never seen before.

yoghurt /jˈoʊgɚt/

a slightly sour custard-like food made from milk curdled by bacteria, often sweetened and flavoured with fruit

Example: I eat yoghurt every morning for breakfast because it is a good source of protein and helps with my digestive health.

yoke /jˈoʊk/

a wooden frame with a bar put across the necks of two animals to hold them together so that they can be worked as a team

Example: The plough was attached to the yoke, which was then placed on the necks of the two oxen.

yokel /jˈoʊkəl/

a person who lives in the country, especially one who appears simple and old-fashioned

Example: The snobbish city dwellers made fun of the yokels who came to town for the state fair.

yolk /jˈoʊk/

the yellow part in the middle of an egg that provides food for the developing embryo

Example: When baking, it is important to separate the egg white from the yolk for certain recipes.

youth /jˈuːθ/

the period between childhood and maturity

Example: When I was in my youth, I had some amazing experiences that helped shape who I am today.

yo-yo /jˈoʊ-jˈoʊ/

a toy consisting of a spool attached to a string, the end of which is held while it is repeatedly spun out and reeled in

Example: When I was a kid, I spent hours playing with my yo-yo, trying to master new tricks and stunts.

yttrium /ˈɪtriəm/

a silvery metallic element used in various alloys and in lasers

Example: The engineers used yttrium as an alloying agent to create a stronger, more durable metal for the aircraft's engine.

Yuan /jˈuːən/

the standard monetary unit of the People's Republic of China

Example: The exchange rate between the Yuan and the US dollar has been fluctuating quite a bit lately.

yucca /jˈʌkə/

a tropical plant with spiky leaves and white flowers

Example: *I am thinking of planting a yucca in my garden because they are low-maintenance and add a nice touch of greenery.*

yuppie /jˈʌpi/

a young highly-paid professional person, especially one who has a fashionable way of life

Example: *I ran into a group of yuppies, all dressed to impress and holding expensive drinks, at the new bar downtown last night.*

Zz

zeal /zˈiːl/

great enthusiasm or eagerness

Example: The cricket team's fans showed their zeal by cheering loudly and passionately.

zealot /zˈɛlət/

a fanatic or an extreme enthusiast

Example: The political activist was a zealot for her cause, always advocating for her beliefs.

zebra /zˈiːbrə/

a black-and-white striped African animal of the horse family

Example: My friend went on a safari in Africa and saw a herd of zebras grazing in the savannah.

zebra crossing /zˈiːbrə krˈɔsɪŋ/

a pedestrian crossing marked by broad black and white stripes

Example: The zebra crossing near my house is always busy during rush hour, with people trying to get to work or school.

zephyr /zˈɛfɚ/

a soft gentle breeze

Example: As the tired teacher sat outside on the porch, she could feel the cool zephyr blowing through her hair and bringing relief from the heat of the day.

zero /zˈiroʊ/

the cardinal number between +1 and -1

Example: Her bank account balance was zero after paying all her bills for the month.

zero gravity /zˈiroʊ grˈævɪti/

the state of weightlessness

Example: Astronauts in orbit around the Earth experience zero gravity, allowing them to float freely in the spacecraft.

zest /zˈɛst/

invigorating or keen excitement or enjoyment

Example: The children squealed with zest and joy as they played in the water park.

ziggurat /zˈɪɡjʊrˌeɪt/

a temple in the shape of a pyramid

Example: The ziggurat was a prominent feature in the ancient Mesopotamian landscape, serving as a place of worship and ritual.

zigzag /zˈɪɡzæɡ/

a line or course having sharp turns in alternating directions

Example: The lightning flashed in a zigzag across the sky, illuminating the entire city for a moment.

zinc /zˈɪŋk/

a brittle bluish-white metallic element that is used in alloys such as brass, to form a protective coating on metals, and in battery electrodes

Example: My grandfather used to work in a factory that produced zinc alloys for various industries, including automotive and construction.

zinnia /zˈɪniə/

a plant of tropical and subtropical America, with solitary heads of brightly coloured flowers

Example: I planted a row of zinnias in my garden this year, and they have added a beautiful burst of color to my backyard.

Zion /zˈaɪən/

the hill on which the city of Jerusalem stands

Example: Many people travel to Israel to visit Zion and other important religious sites.

zip /zˈɪp/

a fastener with two parallel rows of metal or plastic teeth, one on either side of a closure, which are interlocked by a sliding tab

Example: The zip on my jacket is broken and I need to get it fixed.

zither /zˈɪðɚ/

a musical instrument consisting of numerous strings stretched over a flat box and plucked to produce notes

Example: My grandmother used to play the zither every evening to relax.

zloty /zlˈoʊti/

the standard monetary unit of Poland

Example: When I travelled to Poland, I exchanged my dollars for Zloty so that I could purchase souvenirs and snacks.

zodiac /zˈoʊdiˌæk/

an imaginary belt in the sky within which the sun, moon, and planets appear to move, and which is divided into 12 equal areas called signs of the zodiac, each named after the constellation which once lay in it

Example: The zodiac is used by astronomers and astrologers alike to study the movements of celestial bodies and their effects on life on Earth.

zombie /zˈɔːmbi/

a person who appears to be lifeless, apathetic, or totally lacking in independent judgment

Example: After pulling an all-nighter studying for her final Linguistic examination, Annie felt like a zombie the next day, unable to concentrate or think clearly.

a corpse brought to life by witchcraft

Example: My little sister is deathly afraid of zombies.

zone /zˈoʊn/

a region, area, or section characterized by some distinctive feature or quality

Example: The school has a quiet zone in the library where students are expected to work in silence.

zoo /zˈuː/

a place where live animals are kept, studied, bred, and exhibited to the public

Example: The local zoo has a new exhibit featuring endangered species from around the world.

zoology /zuːˈɔːlədʒi/

the study of animals, including their classification, structure, physiology, and history

Example: My friend is majoring in Zoology because she wants to become a wildlife biologist.

zoophyte /zˈuːfaɪt/

any animal resembling a plant, such as a sea anemone

Example: The marine biologist was excited to observe the different types of zoophytes in the coral reef.

zucchetto /zʌkˈɛtoʊ/

a small round skullcap worn by clergymen and varying in colour according to the rank of the wearer

Example: During the Catholic Mass, the priest wears a black zucchetto as a sign of his clerical position.

zucchini /zʌkˈiːni/

a smooth usually cylindrical dark green summer squash

Example: I picked up a fresh zucchini from the farmer's market to make a healthy summer salad.

zygote /zˈaɪgoʊt/

the cell resulting from the union of an ovum and a spermatozoon

Example: The zygote contains all the genetic material necessary to develop into a complete organism.

www.ingramcontent.com/pod-product-compliance
Lightning Source LLC
LaVergne TN
LVHW091623070526
838199LV00044B/909